THORN

AND ITS ENVIRONS

A SOCIAL HISTORY

Graham

Stuart J. McCulloch

ISBN 1-900489-40-6

Published by the Munro Trust in association with Stirling Libraries
Printed by SUNPRINT, 38 Tay Street, Perth PH1 5TT

Frontispiece:	Sketch of Norrieston by Miss Graham.
Front Cover:	'Thornhill' by Henry Morley (1869 - 1937) courtesy of the Smith Art Gallery and Museum

CONTENTS

PART ONE: THE EARLY YEARS

PART TWO: THE GROWTH OF THORNHILL

PART THREE: THE VICTORIAN ERA

PART FOUR: THE TWENTIETH CENTURY

To Gavin and Ruth

Best wishes

LIST OF ILLUSTRATIONS

THORNHILL AND ITS ENVIRONS

A SOCIAL HISTORY

What is the connection between 39 Steps, The Panama Canal, Logarithms and a Tuneless Piper?

READ ON

Foreword

It is all too easy for the passer - by to rush through the village of Thornhill as the hills of the Trossachs beckon impatiently to them. Perhaps the handsome cottages and houses lining the Main Street hardly get a second glimpse. However behind the facade of the white and grey stone houses lies a tale. Not a tale of earth shaking events or of the lordly and great, but of the many small events and the real people who have built the rural community of Scotland.

When I came to stay in the village a few short years ago my initial perceptions, perhaps those of the passers-by above, were quickly corrected. I found a lively integrated community, happy to welcome newcomers yet complete in its self confidence. When research unearthed details of the foundation of the village three hundred years ago plans quickly unfolded for a year long series of celebrations and activities. As a result, I agreed to compile a history of our community to coincide with the year of the Tercentenary.

Primary sources, principally from the Central Regional Council, The Scottish Records Office, Edinburgh and The Central Region Archives in Stirling and Perth yielded a great deal of information, as did the excellent University of Stirling Library and the Smith Museum. I gratefully acknowledge all the help received from the staff at these locations and I must particularly thank Elma Lindsay, Local History Officer, Stirling Council and Lorna Main from the Central Regional Council Archaeological Services.

Every community has a rich seam of historical data just waiting to be discovered and Thornhill is certainly no exception. Many of the long term residents gave invaluable help in providing information. I cannot list all the helpful people that have given advice, assistance and encouragement but I must record my particular thanks to Ian Bain, Jean Buchanan, Cissy Craig, John Dick, Mary Diggins, William Dawson, Tona Fitches, Annie Taylor, Hamish McLachlan, John Millar, Robin Price, Betty Spence, Donald MacFarlane and Betty Paterson. During the course of research Mr. Bob Hendry passed away. Bob was one of the genuine village characters with a huge fund of stories. He will be greatly missed by all of us, and I am glad that I was able to record a few of his tales for the future. Mr. and Mrs. Dick of Hillhead gave unselfishly of their time and wisdom and in allowing me to explore the writings of the Reverend Williams when he was the UF Minister, I was able to gain a great deal of fascinating information collected almost 100 years ago. I am also grateful to Sheila Scott of the Biggar Museum for sharing with me her research on the Buchan family that enabled me to make the connection of John Buchan to Thornhill. For their editing and administration many thanks go to Barbara Thorp, Anne McCulloch, Kirsty McCulloch, William Dawson, Willie Rae and Isobel Rae. Michael Giannandrea of Stirling Libraries has been unstinting in his support and deserves grateful appreciation.

Historical writing is full of dangers and pitfalls, mainly because we are writing about people and events of which we have no personal knowledge. So I have probably made mistakes and for these I apologise in advance. Historical details have been cross checked wherever possible but nevertheless there is a place in this book for oral tales that cannot be substantiated by documentation. I make no apologies for including such tales. A bigger problem is deciding what to exclude and I hope the many contributors will be able to forgive me if have omitted what I should not have. The fault is entirely my own.

As research proceeded certain themes emerged which, I believe, can play a small part in understanding the life of small Scottish communities. The early years brought more than a fair share of conflict and change, because the area enjoyed a position near Stirling, the central 'buckle' of Scotland. Early communications, especially the fords, also tended to direct attention towards the local area. However following the Industrial Revolution the area found itself rather isolated, as the railways became the dominant factor in growth. Therefore there is the opportunity of studying the development of a village built upon long and firm foundations but missing out on the rapid growth that affected many of the small settlements of Central Scotland.

This short history can only introduce the story of the people who have lived and enjoyed the village of Thornhill and the parish community of Norrieston. The pleasure of the unfolding story has all been mine.

Fig. 1 Thornhill Main Street. A general view circa 1900.

An easily recognisable scene today, this looks at the Main Street from the top of The Hill. The new Masonic Lodge dominates the foreground (note the boy without any shoes on the pavement nearby). The War Memorial is not yet built but would occupy the land shown in the bottom left hand corner. The house on the right hand corner of the cross-roads, for a long time a Post Office, has now been demolished. Note the state of the pavements found on The Hill. No doubt it was a matter of considerable scandal for the young lady in the centre of the picture to be riding a bicycle in these pre-suffragette days.

PART ONE: THE EARLY YEARS

1. Secret Paths and Ancient Forts.

A thousand years ago the landscape of this area was very different. Stirling was a far away town accessible from our area only by track and there were no effective roads to open up the area. To the South was the almost impassable Moss of Flanders, an area of thick peat bog containing hidden dangers for the unaware. These frequently flooded areas and secretive marshes effectively cut off the area.

But there was a way across.

To those in the know a hard track led south from the area of present day Thornhill to a crossing point of the river Forth capable of taking a horse drawn vehicle. This crossing point, to be known as the Ford of Frew, would be of considerable significance for future growth.

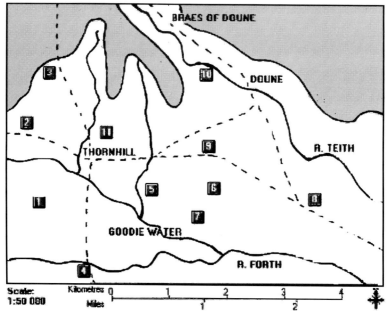

Fig. 2 The Situation and Landmarks around Thornhill

The Kincardine area was in the Western District of Perthshire and formed part of the Stewartry of Menteith. The study area is effectively situated on the land between the Rivers Forth and Teith.

1. Flanders Moss	4. Ford of Frew	7. Craighead	10. Lanrick
2. Tamnafalloch	5. Ballinton	8. Blair Drummond	11. The Skeoch
3. Braendam	6. Coldoch	9. Burnbank	

10

In even earlier years the moss was under the sea with a beach to the North. Thornhill lies on this recognised raised beach at a height of 33 feet. To the North and West lay the mountains of the Central Highlands.

Separating the great moss from the harsh and infertile mountains was an outlier of the Menteith hills forming the narrow ridge by the shore; dry and of promising soil. Although the ground vegetation of birch and thorn scrub made it difficult, it was along this ridge that traffic passed from the North West to the Central Belt, using the only bridge to cross the barrier of the River Forth....situated in the Royal Burgh of Stirling.

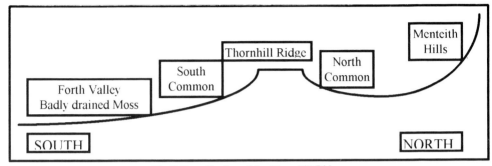

Fig. 3 Cross Section of the Thornhill Ridge

The slight ridge dominating the Moss and the Frews gave a dry platform for future building and development.

In short the area to become the District and Parish of Kincardine, and later the Parish of Norrieston and the village of Thornhill, was strategically well placed in Scotland.

History was not going to pass it by.

Numerous cairns testify to the ceremonial burial of local celebrities, but few now remain. There is an enclosure at Spittalton, now only seen as a crop mark, and at Craighead a further enclosure may represent the remains of a palisade. A possible Iron age Dun (fort) has been identified at Easter Tarr and nearby is a small iron age fort at Tamnafalloch, Ruskie (see fig. 7). This was part of a local group with two further forts at Easter Torrie and Brackland Glen by Callander, forming a neat little defensive position.

Similarly there is little trace left of the Roman outpost on Keir Hill at Auchensalt Farm and the probable temporary Roman camp at Netherton. Yet it is known that a rudimentary Roman Road passed through the local area, from Stirling to Gartmore, in the abortive attempt by the Romans to subjugate our land.

In the far North and the Outer Isles there are numerous remains of mysterious circular structures known as Brochs. These were up to 60 feet high and contained a circular courtyard in the centre with passages and rooms built in the huge thickness of wall enclosing this centre. Their origins are unclear and even the dates of construction are open to debate. Some researchers date them as early as 300 - 350 BC but most have indicated more recent times, perhaps at the end of the Roman Occupation or even during the Viking

11

invasions. What we do know is that they indicate a dangerous time when the possibility of attack was ever present. Local inhabitants on hearing of invasion would flee to their Broch where (they hoped) they would have a measure of protection against the marauders.

Inner galleries

Wooden gallery

Large chamber

Well

Fig. 4 A Broch Reconstructed:

This is what Coldoch Broch may have looked like. It would have supported a large family and retainers for several weeks, having its own water supply and storerooms for grain. The entrance is through a low tunnel and could easily be sealed. The design of Coldoch Broch is almost identical to those found in the Northern and Western Isles, and indicates an early well organised society who communicated ideas and technology over long distances

Brochs are very rare away from the far North and West, yet surprisingly there are at least 3 within 3 miles of Thornhill. One is at Keir (Caer = fort), West Borland, and dates from the Iron Age. There are no visible remains there now but an alleged Iron Age Broch (or possibly a Dun) at Mid Borland is still evident but very much in ruins. However it is a scheduled monument. Broich farm, near Deanston may well indicate the site of a fourth Broch, but the best preserved of all the Brochs is at Coldoch to the South East. This Broch, although in very poor condition, has deteriorated considerably in living memory and testimonies assert that one chamber was still roofed early this century. The circular wall measures between 17 and 19 feet in thickness although it is only five or six feet high now. There are four little chambers off the main centre at basement level and the 2 feet wide entrance was secured by a bar. The slot for this bar is 7 feet deep. An old stairway is still recognisable within the wall. This is now a scheduled ancient monument. It may be that the site of the Broch was coastal when it was built and consequently provided a safe refuge from invaders arriving by sea. Although there is often little to see today these Brochs indicate that the area must have had a substantial settled population, but danger was ever present.

Who provided the threat?

In later years the nearby Highland clans were to enjoy some notoriety, but at this early date the people throughout what we now call Scotland enjoyed a cultural homogeneity, as shown by the sharing of the unique architectural feature of the Broch. Perhaps the invaders were seafarers who were capable of bringing their boats up the Forth. There is no doubt that the Stirling area would have been a good target. Or perhaps, in the days before a unified Scotland under the Dalriadic Scots the invaders would have been the Strathclyde Britons, moving from their capital of Dumbarton and waging war against the indigenous people. A further explanation is that the Brochs were built by collaborators of the Romans and were protection against their own people! It is highly likely that the inhabitants of the Brochs did coexist peacefully alongside the Roman invaders and evidence suggests that the Brochs were burnt following their retreat .

Whoever it was, the people living near the thorn covered ridge would undoubtedly be wishing they would leave them alone, and they would be cursing the River Forth for bringing the unwelcome strangers into their midst.

They were to have more reasons for cursing the river and its convenient crossing place in future centuries.

2. They came to stay

The incoming Scots from Ireland supplanted the local people (probably Picts or Strathclyde Britons) and it was mainly this group who formed the first settled farming communities. Place names in the area reflect the Gaelic speaking origins of many of first local sites, with ancient names such as Cessintully (Seas = a seat or plateau and Dail = meadow). Indeed, many of the Scots names found in the Thornhill area are relatively recent and have superseded the original Gaelic ones, such as Hillhead replacing the much older 'Ballindornich'.

The area, later to become Thornhill, settled into a slow and relatively undisturbed development for a number of centuries. The earliest local records refer to this area as the 'Lands of Thom', mentioned in the Gleneagles Charter, when it was purchased by Sir Walter Menteith. Settled areas include 'Bucopil and Cessintully'. Indeed Cessintully gets another mention when the mill is included in the exchequer rolls of 1480.

The turbulent past of Scotland did not by-pass the area. There would have been outrage at the actions of Sir John Menteith, probably well known locally, when, from his castle in an island on nearby Loch Ruskie, he was accused of treacherously betraying William Wallace shortly after his momentous victory at the nearby Stirling Bridge.

Outrage would have turned to joy when the Highlanders of the North West passed through the area on their way home after their part in Bruce's historic victory of Bannockburn. Seven generations or so later they would have watched an angry Earl of Lennox, with his large retinue, pass through the area following the brutal murder of King James III at the battle of Sauchieburn near Stirling. In 1489 Lennox was moving to Dumbarton to link up with Lord Forbes in order to avenge the murder of his king. He never got there. The party were ambushed in the moss by Lord Drummond's small army accompanied by the young James IV. Lennox was comprehensively defeated and his retinue dispersed.

Descendants of the local people in the following century would have noted with inquisitive interest as the infant Mary, Queen of Scots was spirited through the area on her way to a hiding place on the island of Inchmahome in the Lake of Menteith, well away from her many enemies.

The tumultuous events of the civil wars of the mid 17th century would also have affected the area. The royalist supporters amongst the Highland Clans living around the Trossachs were led by the Marquis of Montrose. They harassed the Cromwellian garrison at Stirling and successfully ambushed a large fighting patrol, sending them scurrying along the ridge back towards Stirling. This would have given much pleasure to James, the 3rd Earl of Perth, living at this time at Burnbank. His son, to become the 4th Earl, was a loyal adherent to Montrose and fought in many of his campaigns. Life would have become difficult for them as a result of the execution of Montrose and the occupation of the district by the Ironsides of Cromwell's army and we hear no more of them living in our area.

14

Fig 5. Loch Ruskie:

This loch is situated to the North West of Thornhill. On an island in the middle (now no longer to be seen) was the stronghold of Sir John Menteith; by repute the man who betrayed Sir William Wallace. The island castle may well have been on an artificial mound constructed in the water and known as a crannog.

3. Norrie and his World

By the year 1200 the area would have been predominantly peopled by Gaelic speaking Scots but over the next 500 years the Gaelic language gradually gave way to Scots English following the cultural and linguistic example of the Scots court in nearby Stirling. This change was consolidated by grants of land made in the area to English speaking Lowland Scots.

One of these Lowland Scots was Robert Norrie, a confidential servant of James I from 1429 - 1437 and later an attendant for his son James II. For services rendered he was given a grant of land in 1482 called the 'Lands of Goodie', soon to be known as Norrieston. Unfortunately Norrie died before he could enjoy the fruits of his labour but the land was passed on to his heirs. James Norrie, probably Robert's son, is mentioned in the exchequer rolls of 1480 and it seems that the fermtoun settlement of Norriestoun, a name still in use today, was well established by 1580. It seems to have been centred to the south of the present village, and present day 'Little Norrieston' and Norrieston Farm mark the original sites.

A town in Scotland was called a 'burgh' and the suffix 'Toun' should not be confused with 'town'. 'Toun' represents the establishment of the Fermtoun, the dominant settlement and economic pattern of much of rural Scotland up to the 18th century. A Fermtoun was a group farm shared by an extended family or by portioners in joint tenure and they were scattered across the landscape. Some of the fermtouns may have grown into small village size but most had only two to four families in principal tenure together with a number of subtenants and cottars. Ramsay of Ochtertyre in his celebrated book 'Scotland and Scotsmen of the 18th Century' said:

> 'as far as records go the Menteith area was divided into towns occupied by 2 or more tenants or cottages built very close together for defence against highlanders'.

4. Hospitals and Healing

By the 17th century the area was well settled with the developing embryonic village of Norriestoun surrounded by a number of fermtouns. Norriestoun (or Knowehead as it was called prior to 1580) was well positioned, being on a loop in the Cessintully Burn by a direct path between the Ford of Frew and the Ford of Lanrick by the Teith.

Mention has been made of the ancient settlements at Boquhapple and Cessintully. A number of other fermtouns were also in evidence and it is interesting that many of their names are a mixture of Gaelic and old English with the suffix 'ton' (a settlement), being common. We have Ballinton (baile - a settlement or town), Munnieston (manach - a monk), Gartincaber (Garrain Cabhar - a grove on a hill side), Coldoch (Coille - a wood and dubh - black), Mollan (Muillean - a mill).

We can now also begin to pick out names of some of those who lived in the area. The spiritual needs of the area were served by a chapel at Boquhapple maintained by the priory of Inchmahome. Associated with the chapel and a reader here in 1584 was Michael Learmonth and by 1594 Alexander Anderson was also involved.

There was an ancient monastery at Kilmadock and this had seven associated chapels. One was called 'Walton'. No trace of this exists today but evidence points to this being situated in the small glen between Boghall Farm and the Mill of Cessintully to the East of the present village. This chapel was still in existence as late as 1720 where it is mentioned in kirk session records. This could indicate that there was a considerable population to the East of the present Thornhill village, but it may simply attest to a central chapel for a number of fermtouns. One of these fermtouns was probably founded by Robert Spittal. Coldoch, the site of the aforementioned Broch, was certainly built by Robert Spittal of Stirling in 1513, although the original mansion house has now been demolished. Robert was the favourite tailor of King James IV and has become famous for the establishment of the hospital at Stirling and the bridges at Doune and Bannockburn. It is likely that the original fermtoun of Spittalton also originates with lands owned by Robert Spittal. He was perhaps attracted and influenced by the site of the small hospital at Spittalton (with a net income of less than £50) which was certainly on the site until at least 1500 AD.

Perhaps a motive for population settling here could be the proximity of Christ's Well. In fact we are unsure of the exact location of this well. Paterson in his 'History of Cambusbarron' maintains that this famous well was the Chapelwell of Cambusbarron, but the Rev. Williams in his extensive research insists that the well was located in the parish of Kincardine and is likely to be associated with an early chapel. Wherever it was it had a huge impact on local people. Men and women for scores of miles around would carry home water in a stoup from this well. This was because it was supposedly endowed with magical healing properties such as giving the power of sight to the blind and the healing of skin disorders - perhaps relating to leprosy.

5. The Tragic Muschets

The estate of Blair Drummond was a powerful influence on life in our area at this time. The first owners were the 'Muschet' family who had come over to England with William the Conqueror and moved to Scotland with Queen Margaret, the anglophile wife of Malcolm Canmore. They were given the lands of 'Kincardine in Menteith' and eventually they rose to high office in the country and were much favoured by the reigning monarchs. Their estate passed to the Drummond family in the 14th century as a result of the marriage of Lady Mary Muschet to Sir John Drummond. The fruits of this marriage were to have enormous implications for the future of Scotland. Their daughter was christened Anabella and she was to become Queen Anabella when she married Robert III (King of Scotland 1390 - 1406). Their eldest son was James I, King of Scotland. Therefore from the union of the Muschet and Drummond families we have the lineal descendants of all the royal house of Stewart, including Mary, Queen of Scots and Charles Edward Stewart or the so-called Bonnie Prince Charlie, much beloved of romantic literature.

Many Muschets remained in the area of Burnbank and Craighead, and were to continue to make their mark, often in a tragic way, on the area. The Craighead Muschets were still in possession in 1752 and at least seven Muschets are recorded in the Craighead deeds between 1632 and 1732. They were indeed a large family. One of their number was Lieutenant-Colonel Robert Muschet who fought with the Prince of Orange in 1681 and may have been involved with the campaigns against the deposed James VII in the North of Ireland.

The Burnbank Muschet's castle of Kincardine, now long gone, was sited approximately where the parish church of Kincardine now stands. A sad aspect of life at this time was the constant fear of the plague. There was no cure and it could strike without warning at any place and time. In the old orchard of Kincardine Castle, near Burnbank today, can be seen a poignant memory to these terrible times: A flat tombstone, and above it a more modern copy, records the death at 26 years old of Margaret Drummond. She was married to George Muschet and along with her three children tragically died near this spot on 10 August 1647.

The plague had taken them all.

The inscription reads:

'Here lyes the Copse of Margaret Drummond, Frid Daughter to the Laird of Invermay, and Spouse to Sir George Muschet of Burnbank, Her Age 26, Departit this Life in the Wisitation with her Frie Children at Burnbank, the 10th August, 1647'

Fig. 6 The 'plague grave' of the Muschets at Burnbank.

The original stone is laid flat but a copy was made in the last century and placed in an upright position above the original. There is now little sign of the orchard in which this grave is said to be situated. The romantic story is that Margaret was buried here because she loved the area so. The more probable truth is that this site was well enough away from the house to avoid the possibility of others being infected.

A further gruesome reminder of these times occurred during road widening at the East end of Thornhill. It was said that the engineers found a number of skeletons when excavating the ground near to the present Lion and Unicorn. A likely explanation for these remains was that this was a grave for plague victims. Its position on the edge of Norriestoun would indicate the desire of the small settlement not to have the bodies buried within its boundary.

A more recent reminder of the danger of disease, this time cholera, is also associated with a Muschet. In the period of the early 19th century cholera was a constant scourge, especially where there was a problem with clean water. Although at this time there was no great problem with clean water in the local area cholera made its appearance nevertheless. A visiting sheriffs' officer of the name Muschet was sadly infected and did not make a recovery. He was buried in an isolated grave at the South East corner of the 'Upper Common' (probably the Skeoch) in order to be well away from the village people and their water supply

He lies there to this day.

6. Rob Roy and the Clan Wars

Disease was not the only concern. The Highland Scots had resisted many of the trends affecting Lowland Scotland and had continued to develop their own clan system. They had gradually moved away from Lowland Scotland in culture, language and tradition. There was frequent enmity between the two areas with Lowlanders often regarding the Highlanders as savages and the Highlanders regarding the Lowlanders as soft and effeminate. Indeed the Gaelic word for a lowlander is 'gall', which can also mean foreigner! The Highland Boundary Fault formed a natural barrier between the two cultures and there was mutual hostility and distrust on both sides of the Highland line. The local area formed part of the border country with a foot in both camps. Internecine warfare was not uncommon, as seen in the 'Battle of Ruskie'. In 1330 the Drummonds and the Menteiths had a bloody conflict at Tamnafalloch ('Hill of Strife'), Tor of Ruskie and many were killed, including three sons of the Earl, Sir John Menteith (of the William Wallace infamy). This feud, no doubt involving many local families, only ended in 1360 when the two parties signed a peace treaty at Stirling.

Further evidence for this conflict came in the 19th century when several gravestones were found, one with the initial PS. Earlier still in the 18th century a sword and coat of mail were discovered on the same site.

The centre for the Menteith family may well have been at Mid Borland where there can be found an alleged post-Norman motte with some visible remains.

The Reverend Williams writes of another clan battle very similar to the previous one and there could be some confusion between the two. However this later clan skirmish took place in the mid 16th Century. The Stewarts of Appin were returning from Stirlingshire via the Vale of Menteith. It was a long journey and they were feeling rather hungry when they stumbled across a wedding feast being laid out. It was bad luck for them that the Earl of Menteith had been invited to the said wedding. The Stewarts tucked into the feast but the Earl himself was less than amused. Menteith pursued the Stewarts up onto a ridge above the Lake of Menteith and there they had an engagement. The Earl and most of his followers were killed; Donald Stewart, the clan chief, only managed to escape under the cover of night accompanied by just one follower.

Fig. 7 Tamnafalloch

There is now little to be seen on this site, although its magnificent position at the top of the ridge overlooking the moss makes it an obvious defensive site. The earthwork mound is now grassed over but can be clearly seen to the left of the picture, and can easily be traced on the ground. This is the site of the clan battle between the Menteith Grahams and the Drummonds and may be the site of the later skirmish involving the Stewarts of Appin and the Menteiths.

In later years, relations with nearby clans were equally strained, especially with regard to the Clan Gregor. The Macgregors, following a number of disagreements with the crown, tended to operate in a semi lawless capacity. It was not uncommon for raiding parties to descend upon the more fertile carse lands and the lands of Lennox to the West, in search of cattle, or to give 'protection' by the infamous 'mall dubh', or blackmail as it has become in English. We have few specific records of raids in Thornhill or the Norrieston area but nearby areas such as Kippen and Gartmore habitually suffered.

An inquiry held at Holyrood in 1585 had the following subject matter:

> *'For samekle as his king's majesty and the Lords of his Pryvy Council*
> *are creditably informed that his good and peaceable subjects inhabiting*
> *the country the Lennox, Menteith, Struilingschyre, and Stratherne are*
> *heavily opressed by reif, stouth, sorning and other crimes dayly and*
> *nightly used upon them by certain theives, lymmers, and sorners lately*
> *broke loose upon them furth of the braes of the countries next adjacent'*

One local example was reported by Ramsay of Ochtertyre. Robert Buchanan of Moss Side described to him how, in about 1640, his grandfather's house was plundered by Macgregors and he was taken prisoner and hidden on a hillside above Callander. Lord George Drummond raised a possee of local men and set out to rescue him. The rescue was successful and without further incident, but serves to demonstrate how in some aspects the local area must have been very like the frontier wild west towns of the USA.

No doubt the frequent passage of clansmen through the area to the lowlands and to the market at Doune would have been a continuing source of tension to the now solidly Scots lowland community. The area is littered with reminders of the days of Rob Roy Campbell MacGregor. As a leading member of the infamous 'Lennox Horse' he offered the dubious privilege of being protected from cattle reivers. He himself was no mean cattle reiver as can be seen in the famous 'hership' of Kippen. In 1691, Rob Roy and his men captured 200 head of cattle and attacked Kippen in passing, adding all its cattle to their haul. However as they were fording the Forth at Frew a detachment of dragoons surprised them. Although battle was joined the highly trained dragoons were routed by the Highland men. Rob Roy would have cause to thank the Frew area a few years later following his altercation with the Duke of Montrose over the loss of £1000 Scots by his chief drover. Rob Roy was outlawed, lost his holdings and land and was continually searched for. He was finally captured somewhere in our area and was tied up and taken towards Stirling via the Frews. Somehow he managed to cut his ropes and he leapt off the horse into the Forth at Frew and so made one of his most famous escapes.

In 1750 the wild streak in the Macgregor family came back to the surface when Robin Oig Macgregor, Rob Roy's son, along with his brother and others, rushed into a house at Edinbilly, Balfron and presented guns, swords and pistols, to the terrified family. They then tore a young 20 year old girl, Jean Kay, from her mothers' arms and bore off with her despite the screams and protestations. Afterwards a forced marriage took place at Rowardennan. The country was outraged and finally Robin was apprehended near Gartmore and taken to Edinburgh for trial. James Fairfoul of Braendam was one of the Justices of the Peace who were prominent in the proceedings against him and helped to bring about a conviction, even though Robin's wife was a Graham who came from Wester Boquhapple, a neighbouring house.

Robin Oig was hanged in Edinburgh on the 1 February 1754.

PART 2 THE GROWTH OF THORNHILL

7. Thornhill gets on the Map.

As in all parts of rural Scotland most of the land was held by relatively few people and these landowners had the absolute authority to feu out their land to new settlers.

The power of the lairds was therefore considerable. A local laird was Archibald Napier, a grandson of the famous John Napier, mathematician and inventor of logarithms. The

Napiers acquired the estate of Kings Boquhapple and the 'Lands of Thom' in April 1617 by purchase from Archibald Edmonstone. The family were certainly occupying local land by 1620 when John's son Robert lived at Boquhapple and wrote a well-known treatise on Alchemy. Archibald Napier, grandson of John, had tasted tragedy in his life when his brother was killed by the Camerons in a clan dispute, but he found happiness when he married Annabel Linton in the year 1679 and moved into Ballinton.

Fig. 8 Ballinton

Above the lintel at Ballinton can be seen the coat of arms of the Napier family and the initial A N for Archibald Napier. Ballinton now has an international reputation for the breeding of highland ponies.

Archibald Napier was a man of considerable local influence as is mentioned in the Acts of Parliament of 1689. William and Mary had acceded to the throne only the previous year ousting the exiled James VII. Many of the Jacobite clans had been in an open revolt which ultimately led to the battle of Killiecrankie, and general insurgency was feared throughout Scotland:

'country of Monteith and places adjacent on both sydes of the river of Forth, that the foords and ferries of the said river above stirling be guarded and secured......do grant full power warrand and commission to Archbald Naper of Boquhaple and James Stewart of Ardvorlich to raise and convocate in armes.............................And to seaze upon and secure all persones, who are lyable to the suspition of being disaffected, or in opposition to the government....'

and:

'Government to Archibald Napier and Stewart of Ardvorlich to raise 300 men to defend the Frews. One half barrel of powder to be provided from Stirling Garrison'

Matters appeared to get calmer in the 1690's and Archibald's thoughts turned to other matters. He obtained permission by Act of Parliament in 1695 to have a weekly market on Thursday and 4 free fairs on 20 October (Margaret's), 14 November (Martinmass), 1st Tuesday in March (Lentron) and 2nd Tuesday in June (Hill's) each year, each one to last 8 days:

'That in all time coming here be four fayrs settled and established yearly at the Toun of King's Balquhaple in the parochin of Kincardine

The right to exact 'toll and custom' was granted to our friend Archibald. All he now needed were some people to make his mercats and fairs a financial success. The markets began operating in 1696, and by 10 February of the same year he began to tackle his people problem by granting fifteen feus of land, located on the 'thorn covered ridge', to new settlers.

We cannot be sure of his motives in feuing this ground, but it is likely that he needed the income. Perhaps it was to maintain his small army, or he may have seen the value and potential of the 'thorn covered ridge' as a market centre. Also possible were other factors that were prominent at the time. In the last years of the 17th century there was a long period of appalling weather which became known as the 'little ice age'. This was to play a major part in the series of appalling famines that were to affect almost all parts of Scotland in 1695 and the following years. Poverty was very much in evidence and it is unlikely that Napier's tenants would have been spared the general hardships throughout the land.

A more intriguing possibility was an involvement in the Darien scheme. This was the ill fated attempt by the Scottish parliament to found a colony at Darien, near the site of the present day Panama Canal. The capital needed for this endeavour was enormous and there was a huge patriotic movement in Scotland to support the venture. In the process it came close to bankrupting the country when the speculation failed. Three Napiers contributed funds. Archibald was not mentioned by name but may well have been involved with other family members in a consortium.

Does Thornhill owe its origin to an attempt to raise capital for the first Scottish colony?

Whatever his motives, Napier can justly claim to have established the village of Thornhill when he feued his plots on either side of what is now the Main Street. His new village was one of the first of a series of planned villages throughout Scotland in Georgian times, but in the initial phase building was on a small scale. The feus were of a standard size of 21 ells (65 feet) wide by 66 ells (203 feet) long or ratios of this size, and initially were fronting the new 'High Street'. It was not initially called Main Street because it was not the *main* road of the time. The existing 'main' route (because it would hardly warrant the term road) ran to the North of the present Main Street, linking up the corner of the church land at Norrieston with the Aberfoyle Road and following the approximate line of the present path through the North Common.

It is difficult to accurately place the first feus in their present geographical setting. Dixon (1995) arrived at a feuing plan based on the premise that the present 'cross lanes' at 50 and 47 Main Street today held the same position in 1696, thus giving a recognisable point to begin placing the feus as entered in the register of Sasines:

'the wynd lyeing South and Northward throwgh the toune of Thornehill'

It is debatable whether these wynds are in the same position today as they were in 1696, especially the Loan on the North side leading to the North Common. However it is a very useful starting point. Initial feus were taken from these central points to the base of the ridge to the East, and from these we can discover the 'pilgrim fathers' of Thornhill.

James Spittal and his wife Agnes McKean took up a large feu at the base of the ridge towards the march with Norriestoun. This plot contained several other existing buildings.

Other first day feus were:

On the south side from the Loan eastwards to the Spittal feu:

- James Law (Kings Boquhapple)
- John Spittal (Kings Boquhapple) shoemaker
- Donald McLaren (Kings Boquhapple) weaver
- Duncan Smith (Bridgend of Doune)
- Robert Sands (Cardross)
- John Maxwell (Murdieston) Notary
- Robert Paterson (Burnside)
- James McCulloch (Murdieston)
- Andrew Chalmers (Mill of Cessintully)

Immediately West of the Loan was

- John Mitchell (Wester Boquhapple)

On the North Side running eastwards from the 'cross' lane was

- Thomas Paterson (McOrriston)
- William Paterson (Boghall)
- William Mitchell (Kings Boquhapple)
- Andrew Mitchell (Kings Boquhapple)

A few other feus were granted in this year including two to John McCullochs west of the loan on the North side and also to David Turner in a spot:

'commonly called Back o' the hill'

Although this marks the formal beginning of the settlement we know as Thornhill there was considerable settlement already in the area in the existing fermtouns. Hearth taxes (levied in 1694 for hearths in permanent dwellings) showed that Boquhapple (Kings), Boquhapple (Western) and Norrieston each had nine permanent dwelling houses, often accommodating multiple tenancies. Most of the first feuars were local people.

Which is the oldest house in Thornhill?

The Lion and Unicorn Hotel by repute dates from 1635 and therefore predates the formation of Thornhill and indeed could claim to be one of the oldest inns in Scotland. This is quite possible as coaching inns tended to be spaced regularly to enable changes of horses to be made and there would have been an early need for such an inn near this site. The present building would probably be on the site of James Spittal's feu of 1696. It is not recorded as such although it is recognised that buildings did exist already on this feu. However it is difficult to date with substantiated proof the oldest house in the village. At the end of the last century a house occupied by a Mr Jenkins was known to have been feued from Archibald Napier in 1696 and was therefore one of the twelve original feus of Thornhill. The central portion of Main Street appears to have the oldest pedigree but there were scattered feus to the west and east. 2 Low Town is said to date from 1701. Hillview also lays claim to be an early feu and its position at the 'top' of the village would give some geographical credence to the claim, despite some doubt about village expansion as far as the hill until the second half of the 18th century. There are a number of other houses of 18th century origin on the Main Street and the Hill and they may also have claims. Springfield, on the Callander Road, once lay astride the old through road to the North of the village and by repute was a Drovers Inn in the 18th century. The oldest house in Norrieston still in present day use appears to be Norrieston House and the adjoining Heatherlea, situated across the road from the Church. Its position in Norrieston, by the site of the old Chapel of Ease, would agree with an early origin, and the deeds of the present day house show that ownership was transferred from James Montgomerie, Tailor, to John Steuart (a common early spelling) in 1757. Therefore the house construction was certainly earlier than this date. The house known as 'Pipers Cottage' at the eastern entrance to the village also predates 1745, as probably does Little Norrieston. The Thornhill record seems to lie with 61 Main Street, for which deeds are still extant giving a date of 1749. Further searches through the sasine registers may clarify this position.

In 1695 Mathew Wallace had succeeded to the charge of the parish of Kincardine and it was during his charge that Thornhill began to see real development. There was no permanent church as yet so he preached once a fortnight on land given to the church by Gabriel (Gavin) Norrie and perambulated by order of Parliament in 1653. Ironically Gabriel was one of the first to be buried on this land, now the churchyard, but his life's work provided a real focus for the village growth.

There had been local agitation for a new full church since 1649. After protracted local argument and opposition by the establishment, Thornhill finally got its new church building, the Chapel of Ease built on Norrie's ground, which opened in deep snow on 29 March, 1728.

Diggens

Fig. 9 The Churchyard and Site of the Chapel of Ease

This shows the original land given by Norrie to the community. The main religious house of the area, the Chapel of Ease, was on this site. The corner stones of the original chapel are still found in the churchyard. The earliest graves have been documented (see Appendix 1).

Sands / Diggens

Fig 10. Sorley's Inn

It is claimed that the Commercial Hotel to the right of the photograph is the oldest building in Thornhill. Although known as the Commercial Hotel until relatively recently it shows the wall plaques of the Lion and Unicorn (its present name) high up on the wall. This may indicate an earlier name. 'Commercial' was a popular inn name after the coming of the railways in the mid 19th century but is unusual much earlier. Another possible explanation of the plaques is political, as the symbols would represent support for the Hanoverian kings (as would the name Crown Hotel) during the Jacobite disturbances between 1688 - 1746.

29

8. In the centre of things

The first half of the 18th century was to see little change in the parish of Kincardine. A slowly rising population saw few people moving to the twin villages of Thornhill and Norrieston. However the base for further growth, established in 1696, was further consolidated in this period for three main reasons

- The military road constructed in 1713 to link Stirling to Inversnaid.
- The agricultural change and draining of the moss.
- The trend throughout Scotland to develop new planned villages.

Communications tend to be a dominant factor in urban growth and Thornhill proved to be no exception.

The main economy of the Scottish Highlands was in the rearing and sale of cattle for the rich markets of Southern Scotland and England. This led to the development of the droving trade, in which cattle in large herds were driven 'on the hoof' from the North to the large fairs at Crieff and especially Falkirk. From the North West the main droving routes tended to arrive from Aberfoyle or through the Leny Pass towards where Callander is now situated. From there the cattle would pass over the bridge at Stirling and onto Falkirk. Thornhill was bypassed by the Callander route for a long time, but when the Stirling Bridge tolls increased many drovers took the cheaper option and used the ancient and free fords of Frew south of the village. Thus Norrieston and Thornhill became thriving centres for the droving trade. It was tradition to allow the drovers 'stands' where they could allow their cattle to graze overnight, and several such stands surrounded the village. However the area of the commons was jealously guarded for the sole use of the villagers. Drovers tended to sleep in the open with their cattle but would have made use of the numerous inns in the village for refreshment. The present buildings housing the Crown Hotel and the Lion and Unicorn were in use by this time and it is easy to imagine many a lively night in the various bars.

Thornhill has a long tradition of tolerance to travellers and perhaps the continuation of the droving custom led Thornhill later to become well known as a centre for travelling folk, and hence earn its local reputation as 'Tinkertown'!

The drovers used rough paths and rights of way but there were few roads as we imagine them until one was driven along the ridge about 1713. This was the military road connecting the castle at Stirling to the new fort at Inversnaid and followed the route of the new village settlement. Since 1688 Scotland had been split by serious political rifts between the exiled Stewart kings and the incoming Orange and later Hanoverian monarchs. Most of the Highland Clans in the nearby Perthshire Highlands tended to support the Stewart kings and this led to numerous risings and local difficulties. To 'nip trouble in the bud' the government built a series of forts and garrisons in the heart of the troubled areas. One such fort is at Inversnaid on the banks of Loch Lomond and the ruins can still be seen today.

The redcoat soldiers garrisoning the forts were sometimes Scots (the Black Watch were raised for such duties) but more often than not they were English soldiers. They were sometimes regarded as an army of occupation, particularly as the very unpopular Act of Union had only just been pushed through the Scots parliament in 1707. Locals must have been curious to see the foreign troops frequently marching along the road, but at least new markets opened up and they would have gained some welcome trade.

9. Ye Jacobites by name

The Jacobite rebellions of 1708 and 1715 had a minor impact in the village although locals must have held their breath when the large Jacobite army of the Earl of Mar camped at Kinbuck near Dunblane on the eve of the Battle of Sherrifmuir. They would have watched some of the Macgregor contingent under our old friend, Rob Roy, rushing along the military road towards the battle area. Perhaps many of these participants would have been well known to them from when they came to the new Thornhill fairs with their cattle. The Macgregors paused along the route to capture 20 government guns in and around Callander but stood on the sidelines when the Sherrifmuir engagement took place. We have no evidence of local connections in this rebellion although it is highly likely that there were mixed feelings about involvement.

A bigger talking point emerged just six years after the battle when Nicol Muschet, one of the remaining members of that ancient family, was taken away for the murder of his wife at Boghall. He was later executed in the Grassmarket of Edinburgh.

The smaller but more famous Jacobite rising of 1745 is better documented. Although the army of Charles Edward Stuart rarely rose above 5000 men, it has imposed a rich picture upon our history. In 1746 there were 490 men aged 14 - 60 in the parish of Kincardine and we know that 10 local men were engaged in the Jacobite army and were almost certainly present at the ill fated battle of Culloden. This number is surprisingly small because most of the Drummond family, feudal superiors for much of the village, were heavily engaged with the Prince and James Drummond, the Earl of Perth, was the joint leader of the Jacobite forces. In addition the Haldanes of Lanrick were also active and devoted to the Jacobite cause. The Thornhill volunteers would probably have signed up when the Jacobite Army moved through the area on the day of 12 September 1745 prior to crossing the Forth at Frew in an attempt to miss the heavily fortified bridge and castle of Stirling. They were expecting to be attacked at the crossing by Gardiner's Dragoons, but the dragoons fled back to Stirling at the first sight of the Jacobites! Local tradition tells that Prince Charles spent that night in a house where presently stands Moss side of Boquhapple. This is not true as he slept in the house of MacGregor of Balhaldie in Dunblane. The confusion may have occurred because the grandfather of a Mr. Syme of Mossside did receive a sword from Charles Edward Stuart for the loan of a horse on that day.

It is certain that Charles' advance guard of officers and clansmen were billeted in the main houses in the village and wined and dined at the local hostelries. We know that Duncan McPharrie who commanded a MacGregor company of the Highland army slept this night in Thornhill. Mr. Ballantyne, who lived in 'piper's cottage' at the time recorded that the army commandeered a horse from him. The horse was obviously not a Jacobite because it apparently threw its rider even before reaching the Ford of Frew and then plodded its own way home. Perhaps the horse had sensed the presence of 'calthrops' on the ground. These vicious little pointed iron spikes lie almost invisible on the ground but are quite capable of laming a horse. The Ford had been liberally sprayed with these devices in an attempt to delay the Jacobite army. They probably would have succeeded without the intervention of Robert Forrester of Wester Frew. He knew the way through the lethal spikes and offered to navigate the Prince around the hazards. His offer was gratefully accepted and the Jacobite army moved through this major obstacle on their way to capturing Edinburgh and the successful battle of Prestonpans.

Although not many locals took part in the rebellion it was considered a good spectator sport. Several residents went to watch the battle of Falkirk and were almost caught up in the fighting. James and Henry Grahame of the Brae of Cessintully were less lucky because they were captured. James escaped but Henry was taken north by the Army and was in captivity at the time of the Battle of Culloden.

10. Whales and Moss Lairds.

By 1755 the population of Kincardine Parish, comprising mainly the areas of Blair Drummond and Thornhill stood at 1250 people of which 1248 were Protestants and 2 were Catholics. This information was compiled by Webster in his 1755 census. He also records that the number of fighting men in the district stood at 250. This illustrates the nervousness of the government about a future Jacobite rising only 9 years after the end of the last one!

The Parish of Kincardine was then made up of two sections: the wet carse alongside the rivers Forth and Goodie made up the majority of the land, and a smaller section was made up of the 'dry field' alongside the River Teith and the higher land. From 1750 the population actually began to decline. The fermtouns were becoming outdated and the smallholdings, really no more than crofts, were hardly viable units. It has been recorded that in the late 18th century the state of agriculture in West Perthshire was still primitive. Four tenants often had one plough gang between them and each sent one man and one horse to the spring ploughing. The four horses were yoked to a broad plough. One man held the horses, one drove them, one held the plough and the fourth dug rocky areas where the plough could not go. The land was then divided into small parcels about 18 feet square for which the tenants cast lots. Hazel or willow rods marked the borders of their allotted plots and each sowed their seed. It was then noted that the rest of the year until harvest was spent by the group feuding about their boundaries!

Returns on the land were poor and agriculture was barely economic. The infield land was quite good and well manured but the outfield was poor. In summer, peat was dug and burnt for fertiliser. The fields everywhere were in run-rig similar to the system described above. The main, and in some cases the only crop, was black oats. The run rig system was virtually obsolete in our area by the mid 1700's and the great enclosure movement was gathering force as the common land and outfields began to get enclosed for arable. The myriad of small farms then became amalgamated into larger and more economic holdings. The pattern of surrounding farms began to look more like that which can be seen today. Some of the dispossessed peasant farmers moved into the small village of Thornhill and began to develop industries and services for the surrounding population. Many moved away completely to supply labour for the cities that were beginning to sprout in size as the industrial revolution entered its introductory phase. The local population loss was short lived as another event, which was to capture the imagination of the nation, changed the local landscape in a dramatic fashion.

Despite the present 'set aside' policy of the European Community we would have looked at the landscape then and have been amazed at the amount of land not in cultivation. Many areas had remained almost unchanged from the dawn of civilisation and one of these areas would have been the great moss that covered all the headwaters of the Forth. 3000 years ago this area was a secluded arm of the ocean and formed a shallow sea. Fine muds were being laid down in the quiet waters and further proof of the sea presence can still be seen in the frequent beds of shells found on the carse. One very thick bed was found at the Bridge of Goody. Also, in 1824, the bones of a large whale were found near Coldoch and were kept in a museum in Blair Drummond. Falling sea levels led to this area becoming land and it was soon occupied by a thick layer of forest with oak, hazel, alder, birch and willow. Some of the oak trees were immense and during clearing in 1793 we are told that one oak trunk was 4 feet 8 inches in diameter and in 1823 another was found which reached 16 feet in circumference. It appears that the forest was felled by Agricola during the brief Roman occupation of the area, probably because it gave such good shelter to the pugnacious Caledonians in its midst. The whole area is still only a few feet above sea level and it gradually developed, in our wet climate, a thick bed of wet peat which was virtually useless for agriculture. However, it was realised that underneath the peat was available agricultural land. The only problems were to get rid of the peat and to keep the existing land dry by good drainage. This problem was to be solved by the genius of Lord Kames and helped on its way by a large surplus labour supply.

The labour supply was a direct result of the 1745 rebellion. Many of the clans of Perthshire were solidly Jacobite, and they suffered heavily in the aftermath of the rebellion. Most of the leaders lost their land and the ordinary people found that the paternal clan system was broken, never to return. The overcrowded Highlands could no longer support such a large population in the prevailing peaceful environment and many looked towards the nearby lands for work. The Balquhidder area was one of the dispossessed estates following the 1745 Rebellion and was to provide a significant number of the new settlers. They found their new work in the clearing of the moss.

The settlers were called moss tenants, or very often the tongue in cheek, 'moss lairds'. Initially they were treated with considerable hostility and often they were considered to be 'undesirable aliens'. The scheme to drain the moss was treated with derision and was doomed to failure in the opinion of many local residents!

The 'moss lairds' were given a 36 year lease as standard. Initially the terms for work seemed rather good for the time. They received money and timber to build a hut and paid no rent for 7 years. Then they faced a mounting and crippling scale of rental, all for the backbreaking job of stripping the low moss through sheer hard work and muscle power. They had to live in very damp conditions. The first house was only turf or peat but their second was usually of timber or brick (from the nearby Blairdrummond new brick works).

As time went on however, the egalitarian people of Thornhill considered them to be very hard done by in giving what they saw as essentially sweated labour for the landlords. Not all agreed, and the area of moss cleared, and the number of settlers on the moss gradually increased. The first areas of moss cleared were to the East of Thornhill on the estates between Blair Drummond and Stirling. Soon clearance spread to the moss to the South of the village. The early ways to clear the moss lay in digging a trench down through the peat to the clay below. This trench was made into a channel that ran North to South and led into the Goody or the Forth rivers. The tenants would loosen the peat either side of the channel and throw peat into the water to be taken away downstream. However this relied upon an abundant source of water and this was not always present. The first tenant took up the enterprise in 1767 but by 1782 there were 42 families working on the moss, 37 of them from the Perthshire Highlands.

In 1783 the drainage venture took a more dramatic turn, especially in the Blair Drummond section, and events there were to have an impact on agricultural development throughout the world. Lord Kames had married Mrs Agatha Drummond of Blair Drummond and hence acquired the large Drummond Estates. He turned his fertile brain to the problem of creating equally fertile land and in 1783 began stripping the peat using flowing water. A local engineer, George Meikle from Alloa, won a contract to design a huge wheel capable of lifting large volumes of running water from the Teith up to a height of 17 feet, and it was installed at the Mill of Torr.

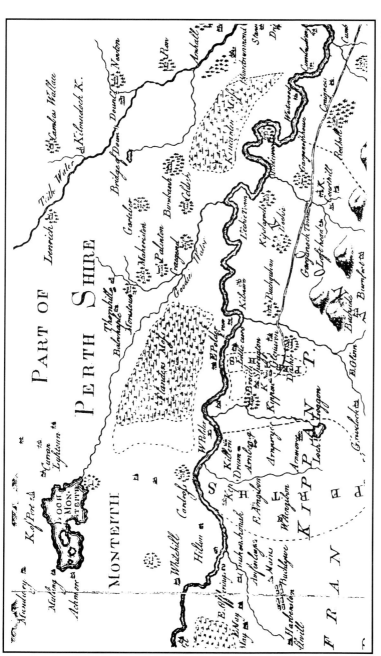

Central Regional archives

Fig. 11 Edgar's Survey map 1745

One of the first available maps. It is not strictly accurate but gives a good impression of the area at this early date. Thornhill and Norrieston exist separately but both appear to be very small. The main surrounding houses such as Lanrick, Garteber (Gartincabar), Palinton (Ballinton) and Coldoch are shown. No road yet links the area to Stirling (the military road is not shown) but a road does go from Stirling to Kippen. Note the very large extent of the Kincardine Moss and Flanders Moss. Thornhill would have been a very remote community at this time.

Fig. 12 The 'Meikle' Water Wheel

The wheel, designed by George Meikle, was set up at the Mill of Torr by Blair Drummond. It turned continuously for over 40 years until 1840, lifting the water from the Teith to the Forth Drainage Basin.

In 1787, water diverted in this way ran south across huge channels through the moss. Trenches were dug parallel to each other and the water floated off the (previously loosened) peat into the Forth creating arable land.

However, much of the work was still done by the hands of the local tenants and labourers. Lord Kames became one of the first large scale 'improvers', introducing many other new methods and ideas as the farms were consolidated and the tenants offered longer leases.

He was not the only one. A Mr. McEwan of Black Dub farm was recorded as being 'noted for intelligent enterprise'. He invented the successful Drain Plough and put it to good use on his land. The drainage of the area immediately to the South of Thornhill saw Messrs. Sim, Paterson and Doig, all local men, carrying on the work of Lord Kames. In the process almost all the common land, with the exception of the North and South Common and high up on the Skeoch, was taken into private ownership. But it was not without a fight. There are records of a serious dispute in 1806 over the Commonty of Boquhapple Moss or the Poldar Moss consisting of 438 acres between the Goodie and the Forth. Lord George Drummond was opposed by John Paterson, John McCubbin and John Buchanan. The result of this legal dispute is unclear and could be called a draw. However, it was to last nine years and provide a test case for the future into the rights of the smaller tenant farmers in dispute with the large landowners. Nevertheless by 1816 the whole area was divided and the common ground lost.

However the area to the West of the village has never been cleared and now forms the protected Flanders Moss, giving us an insight into what the whole area from Stirling to the headwaters of the Forth once looked like prior to its drainage.

11. The Early Village.

It is now possible to begin to construct a picture of Thornhill in the late 18th century. The parish of Kincardine had a population of 2068 people and Thornhill, the largest settlement (Thornhill and Norrieston had now joined together) had reached a population of some 626 people. Along with many other places in West Perthshire there had been a growth of planned villages and towns in the later years of the 18th century replacing the more dispersed rural community. Callander, Crieff, Muthill, etc. are all local examples of planned villages. However Thornhill is almost unique in having maintained its original planned layout of a straight main street with feus extending north and south.

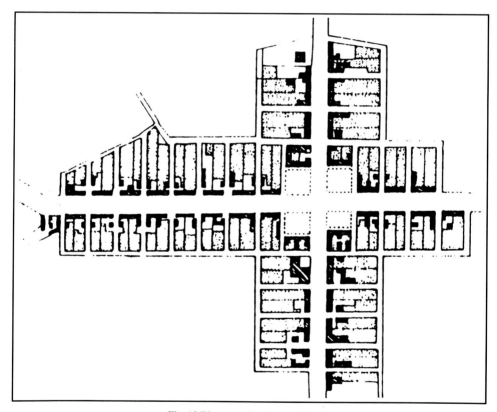

Fig. 13 Diagram of a planned village

The cruciform shape was the most popular of the designs for the Georgian planned village. Thornhill broadly follows this pattern with a dominant Main Street and a Cross Roads. Note the broad open space at the Cross which was intended to be a Market Place. Thornhill never developed the open market space, but in other respects it is very similar to the outline plan especially with the long evenly spaced feus behind the houses.

The feus gave enough space for growing potatoes and other crops and the keeping of a limited number of animals. Most of the early residents were virtually crofters, using the strips to the rear of the houses for arable, and grazing cattle on the common grounds. The barns and byres, most now used as sheds, are still in evidence to the rear of many of the houses on the Main Street and the Commons are still found both North and South of the village. The South Common is now used as a football park and children's playground. The North Common maintained its original function as a common grazing area until quite recently and is now valued as an area of open space for the villagers. Further Commons existed to the North of the village (the Skeoch) and down on the Moss lands but these have since been lost.

In a survey of 1771 the main landowners in this district were (value of estate given in Pounds Scots) :

	Pounds
Lord Kames of Blair Drummond	3072
Murdoch of Gartincaber	66
Graham part Boquhapple	193
Govan as above	125
Drummond as above	26
Laird of Craighead, Norrieston	229
Earl of Moray (Coldoch, Mill of Goodie)	342

Most of the people in the village were labourers or artisans. Tanning was an important industry employing 20 men, producing shoe leather for export. The tannery was situated west of the site of the present Robert Dykes Garage but is now no more. Some were employed in the new Deanston Adelphi Cotton Mill. This was beginning to grow at a tremendous rate and employed over 700 people in the early 1790's. The whole area was growing fast and the 1801 census recorded a population of 2212 people in the parish, a 10% increase in 20 years.

12. The Effects of Married Life

All was not rosy, as the area had developed a bad reputation for rheumatism for people of middle age, especially incomers, due to the damp climate. It seemed to have less effect on the locals. We hear of the Earl of Moray speaking to his tenants in the Frews area in the 17th century. He saw tenant John dancing merrily on a table at the age of 70 and he said in jest:

> *"John you are too rich and wanton. I must raise my land (rents)"*.

John answered:

> *"My lord, it is not the land that has made me rich, but god's providence...... and the change of wives!"*.

Nevertheless, for most people, life would have been hard and very simple. Visitors were surprised by the total lack of servility that seemed part of the make up of the Scottish peasantry, unlike the almost total control exerted by the upper classes of England. However, we had little to be proud of in terms of material possessions.

Early visitors to Scotland often remarked that they were puzzled by the apparent disregard of local people for material possessions, noting especially the poverty of the houses. Froissart reported in 1385 that Scots were largely unconcerned by the burning of their homes in the English Wars, as they said they could rebuild them in three days as long as they had some timber for the roof. Three hundred years later the houses were not much improved and most of the houses in the village were little more than hovels. By 1790 there were signs of progress and all of them now had glazed windows.

However the moss houses built by the first settlers were striking indeed. Until the peat had been removed there was little point in erecting brick or stone houses, so, the following method of constructing was adopted:

> *'A deep trench was first cut in the moss and carried down into the clay below the peat. In the centre was left a large block of solid peat the same size as a house. Then the house itself was scooped out of this block, rather like hollowing out a turnip on Halloween. The walls were 4 feet thick at the base and 3 feet at roof level and timber was used for the roof. As the peat dried out the walls contracted so that a room originally 12 feet high ended up as 5 feet high'!*

No doubt this played havoc with the interior decoration schemes! Surprisingly it did not play havoc with health, despite what must have been very damp conditions. Records show that many people in this area were noted for longevity, a tradition carried into more modern times by the MacFarlanes of Crosshill.

Crosshill (or Corshill as it is known today) was a smithy earlier this century, the last smith being Sandy MacFarlane. He died at 94 years old, both his parents lived well into their eighties and his brother Daniel lived to 88, still shoeing horses well into his seventies. His other brother Robert died at the comparatively young age of 81, but Robert's son, also called Daniel broke the family record. He died shortly before his 106th birthday and remained active to the end. He accounted for his longevity by eating plenty of porridge and never marrying. However he was quick to point out that he had had plenty of opportunity but was never tempted.....not even by his housekeeper of 51 years, Miss Anne Alexander. When asked why they did not marry she replied:

"he isn't my type and I'm certainly not his"

(Interview on the occasion of Daniel's 104th birthday.)

MacFarlane

Fig. 14 Crosshill Smithy

A working scene from the inside of the Crosshill (Corshill) Smithy circa 1900. This smithy was the home of the MacFarlanes, so noted for longevity.

42

13. Life and Work in the late 18th Century

There were now 126 moss tenants in the parish together with their families giving a total of 640 people. By 1811, there were 886 people living and working on the moss. These new settlers were almost all Highlanders. They were tough, wore Highland dress, and spoke Gaelic, many not having any English at all.

They were well known for supporting each other and tended to think of themselves as foreigners in a foreign land. However, the image of the wild Highlander was not well founded in this case. It was noted that there was not one reported instance of theft or other misdemeanour amongst them and not one of them claimed Poor Relief. They were known to be sober, frugal and industrious, but there was no Gaelic church or school for them. The Society for the Propagation of Christian Knowledge agreed in 1793 to employ a bilingual teacher to give the scriptures. The teachers contract allowed him or her to live rent free, get a 1/3 acre of Carse land, a school house, a cow and free fuel. Some modern teachers might envy this!

It is noteworthy that in earlier years Thornhill was noted as a centre of Divinity. In 1762, many students of Divinity lived in the parish. By 1790 there were few left in the area, probably because the area had become too expensive for them. However there were two clergymen, a minister of the Parish of Kincardine and a minister of the Chapel of Ease at Norrieston.

A written descriptor of the village noted that:

'Most people are religious, sober, industrious and frugal but several are intemperant, with cases of fraud and stealing. This is because of the effects of distilling local whisky'.

Whisky distilling had became very important, with the Thornhill blend being well known throughout Scotland. It is difficult to establish exactly where the stills were situated as there are very few official records kept of this industry! However there was a legal distillery at Spittalton. The excellent flavour of the local blend was said to be a result of the local water, much of which came from a well at Middleton. This distillery was set up by Robert Downie about the middle of the 18th century, but an Act of Parliament stopped production to allow concentration on the larger commercial distilleries. So ended the Thornhill whisky industry, but Robert Downie was to make his mark elsewhere. It was said that he made his fortune in the developing British Empire Province of Bengal, India and returned to become the local Member of Parliament. This new career did not last long as he was accused of bribery and decided to resign his position. He did not blame his friends and acquaintances in Thornhill and he later presented a fine communion cup to the Chapel of Ease.

The same chronicler who remarked on the evils of whisky drinking also noted that things improved when whisky distilling stopped! Nevertheless there were still seven ale houses in Thornhill and a local minister complained that the inns produced a pernicious effect:

"especially when the innkeepers are low persons"!

It was not all drinking. There was also one parish schoolmaster and five private schools. It was noted that:

'All were well attended in winter but deserted in summer because of the practice of the children working on farms'.

The general impression of the village was, on the whole, favourable. The Reverend Hugh Laird (Minister in 1800) left Thornhill to take a charge in Portmoak and one day met Mr. MacFarlane of Whirriston. He complained:

"Oh, it was a fine place - Thornhill. Plenty of respectable men for elders - here I can get only tailors or shoemakers".

The reverend gentleman had obviously not received very many favourable comments about his dress sense!

By the early 1800's Thornhill had virtually become self supporting. There were over 40 looms in the village and it was said that almost every house was:

'enlivened by the sound of the loom'

In addition there were six to eight shoemakers, nine tailors, two coopers, a saddler, four nailers and several smiths and millers, with at least two working mills at Cessintully to the East and the Mollans to the West. In addition there was a woollen mill near the Cessintully Mill to service the looms. A lot of soft fruit was grown in the fields around the village giving casual work for young people. There were now two schools, both ultimately to be replaced by the present school building. Thornhill was not a wealthy community but there were few very poor people either, with only three families maintained by the parish.

A major issue of the time was transport and there was strong local pressure to improve the appalling condition of the roads. An early map of the area was by James Stobie in 1783 and it showed that there was a road of a kind through the village. There was no road linking the now sizeable settlement at Low Town to the Main Street, and Doig Street did not exist although there were some weavers' cottages there. Equally there was no road to Frew and Kippen apart from the tortuous route via Cessintully Mill and Ballinton. The main route from the North came from the Lanrick Ford over the Teith and into the West End of Thornhill, probably where the North Common joined the Callander Road. Unfortunately this road has now disappeared but certain parts of this route are still rights of way today. The route into Stirling was completely different at Blair Drummond and the main route basically followed the path of the Teith as far as Drip Bridge. The Road between Callander and Thornhill was said to be barely passable, and quite impossible in winter. The road South to Frew was not much better. The draining of the moss had another useful spin-off when a new turnpike road was constructed along the North side of the moss thus helping Thornhill to communicate with Stirling. When other new roads were constructed in the early 19th century it must have been a revelation to the formerly isolated villagers, although no doubt visits to Stirling would have still been infrequent and a rather special occasion.

Fig. 15 Weavers Cottages, Low Town.

McLachlan

Thornhill had a thriving domestic weaving community, especially in Low Town and Doig Street, for almost 100 years. The cloth was woven in the home. The rise of the factory system in the late 18th century and early 19th century led to the demise of the home weaving industry. The weavers' revolt of the early 1800's led to the crushing by force of the weavers who complained of their appalling pay and conditions. Two weavers were hanged in Stirling for their 'crimes' and it is possible that local weavers were involved in this minor revolt. A Perthshire weaver's leader was named Sands, the name of one of the original village feuars, and by now an important family in Thornhill. This photograph dates from the early 1920's and demonstrates the poor state of the road.

Fig 16 William Johnson's Map of Western Perthshire.

An early example of a genuine cartographic attempt to show this area, based on James Stobie's Map of 1783. Thornhill is shown as a distinct route centre at the junction of five routes. Norrieston is no longer shown as a separate village, and the weavers row of Low Town is clearly shown. The main route south is by Craighead and the Bridge of Goody towards Frew. The present road south to Kippen was laid down as a turnpike road in the early 19th century. The route to Callander is similar to today but the main route North was by the Skeoch towards the Ford of Lanrick. Unfortunately this route has now disappeared although a few traces still remain. Note the Chapel of Boquhapple still remains just to the west of the village, Blairhoyle is known as Leitchtown and Hillhead has its original name of Ballindornich.

14. Growth and Change in the 19th Century: The Village

By the mid 19th century Thornhill was developing into a more easily recognisable form for present residents. The major landowners around the village by this time were recorded as Messrs. Paterson, Doig, Duncanson, and Moir, the last family still holding farming land in the area to this day. The population of the parish had reached an all time high in 1832 of 2245 but was set to decline thereafter. The initial immigration to drain the moss in the previous half century had ceased to be replaced by the spectre of emigration. Numerous local families were destined to make their homes in the emerging colonies, especially Canada.

Religion still played a major part in the village as it did throughout Scotland. By the 19th century the Chapel of Ease was in a very poor state of repair. Local tradition says this is because it was set on fire in the late 18th century. It is said that a passing soldier on his way to Inversnaid fired a shot into the church that ignited the building and almost burned it to the ground. Whether or not this was a deliberate act of vandalism we shall never know. However tradition has it that he paid his penalty when his horse inexplicably reared near the Boquhapple Road End and threw him. His skull shattered on meeting the ground and he rose no more! The chapel was repaired by 1815 but the work was never fully completed.

In the early years of the century the small chapel of Boquhapple still stood by the side of the road about half a mile outside Thornhill on the Aberfoyle road. It was rarely used and was to drift out of the local history similar to the chapel of Walton.

The road layout was roughly as it is today although the Main Street (then called the High Street) had become narrower and was not metalled. The Hill (or Hill Street as it was then called) was then a cul de sac. It was still not 'made up' in living memory. Some older residents remembered with amusement the scenes of their childhood as they watched the chaos and listened to the cursing, as horses, vehicles and people tried to climb the Hill in winter when frost lay on the ground. It was even worse when the winter rains turned the area into a quagmire.

The vast majority of the present houses on the Main Street were built by this time although there were many more shops and services. However the number of licensed premises had declined to just two, being the present public houses; the Crown (a listed building), and the 17th century Lion and Unicorn which then bore the name of the Commercial Hotel. The village post office was then situated in a nearby house now called Slatehaa but it was to move location three times over the next 100 years. There were two schools. The present site of the school was in use at this time, although in earlier times Number 2 Low Town, the house across the road, had acted as the main school. This school was operated under the administration of the church but the East School, which was unendowed, was situated where the present car park now stands opposite the Scout Hall.

Sands / Diggens

Fig. 17 Sands' Shop circa 1900, and the Buchan Connection

The two houses to the left were built by Alexander Stewart in the late 18th century, and it is likely that the cottage to the right was also built by him. Alexander Stewart was the great, great grandfather of John Buchan, 1st Lord Tweedsmuir. The shop on the left is called Slatehaa and is by repute the first house in the village to have the luxury of a slated roof. The shop and post office belonged to Mr. Sands, and this family owned a number of properties on the main Street at the turn of the present century. Note the building, now demolished, on the site of the Lion and Unicorn Car Park, and the narrowness of the road at the entrance to the village of Thornhill.

49

The Aberfoyle Road was known as Shuttle Street, reflecting the weaving industry that had become prominent in the village. This is probably where George Spittal had his workshop. Getting bills paid was just as difficult then as now, as shown by a letter sent in 1830 from a Mr. Buchanan to George Spittal:

> *George,*
> *I believe you are in much need of your money and I confess that we should have paid you before now - and we would have done so too - had we money to dispose of - this you may believe for it is a fact. It was not for want of desire then to pay your money but want of money that was the cause of this delay.*

Mr Buchanan offered to pay £7 immediately to be sent by carrier to Doune, and the rest at some time later. Unfortunately we have no details of George's reply but we can imagine it!

Shuttle Street was dominated by the tannery, along with a number of nearby cottages, now mainly gone. A path linked Shuttle Street, as it still does, with Low Town, although Back Yetts was not yet in existence. Nevertheless there were at least four houses along the path by the burn. The Low Town was almost separate from Thornhill with its own distinct community established in the large feus that served as crofts for the inhabitants, a local school and its own water supply from wells. Indeed most of the residents of the village would have been what today we call crofters. Many had other occupations but almost all would have kept a few animals, grown corn and potatoes, and made use of the common grazings around the village. An old map of circa 1812 shows some of the recently parcelled out land on the mosses to the South of the village. Marked clearly are the lines allocated to feuars of Thornhill, Norrieston and others for the cutting of peat. It refers to 'peat rooms' and this may be the lines where peat was to be cut. It may also mean temporary dwellings used by the villagers to stay in when cutting the peat, rather like the shieling type sheds still in use in the Western Isles.

To the South of Low Town was Doig Street. It is likely that this was a new street in the 19th century although some of the houses pre-date this. By 1861 there were seven clear blocks of houses / cottages, perhaps containing up to 18 families. The name of this street reflects an old family in the area who have also given their name to the nearby parish of Kilmadock (the chapel of the dog family). In 1472 Sir Thomas Dog was the Prior of Inchmahome and occupied a prominent position in the area. Gravestones have also been identified of James Dog (1519) and Walter Dog (1631). A Paul Dog was in Cessintully Mill in 1567, and later branches of the Dog family lived in Gartincaber and other addresses in the local area.

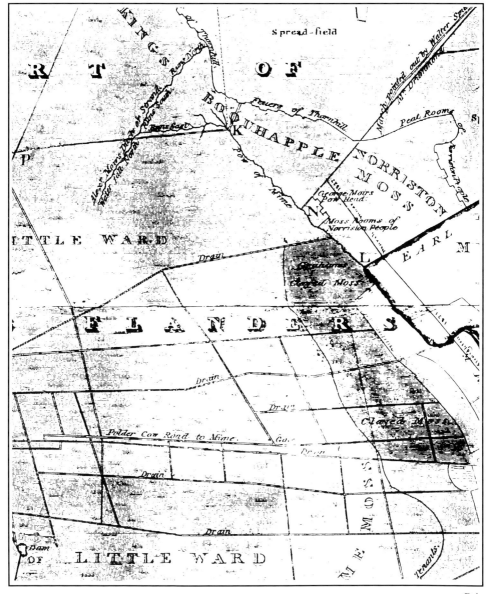

Bain

Fig. 18 Moss Drainage and Common Ground.

This early 19th century map shows the Moss to the South West of Thornhill. To the North are the areas of land parcelled out to local inhabitants. The 'Rooms of Thornhill' and the areas to be used by the feuers of Thornhill are clearly visible as are the 'Moss Rooms and Peat Rooms of the Norriston People.' This area was the site of a legal battle over common ownership of land. The original estates are also shown, such as Kings Boquhapple with Alexander Moir's ditch, Norriston Moss with the March pointed out by Walter Spittal for Lord Drummond, and the estates of the Earl of Moray to the East.

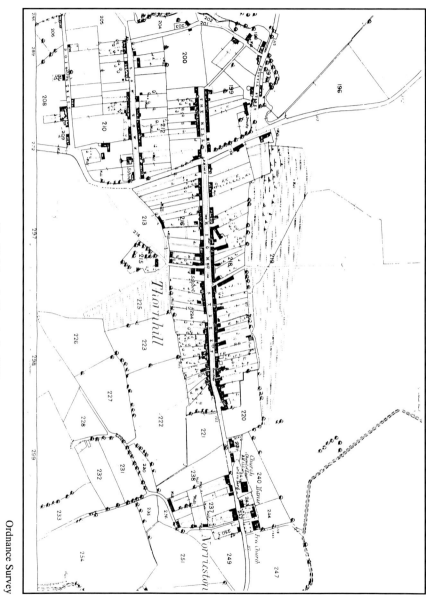

Fig. 19 Map of village in the 1866

Ordnance Survey

The main street of the village was then the High Street, and Shuttle Street with its Smithy is prominent. Note the two schools and the number of wells, especially those at the bottom of the feus by the road and South Common. Norrieston is still a separate settlement to the East

15. 'Second to none for well cultivated farms'

The developments in agriculture on the Carse in the last century had attracted world wide interest and were often used as examples of what enlightened landowners could do to improve their land. They became an element of what we now call the 'Agricultural Revolution'. They were a constituent part of a general but dramatic farming change in which fields were enclosed, new techniques were adopted and marginal land was brought into cultivation. The end result was a decline in the agricultural work-force but a massive improvement in agricultural output. The fertile and varied lands around Thornhill were ideally situated to take full advantage of these improvements. On the 7 January 1823 a cattle market was held in the village. Although the right to have fairs had been granted to Thornhill in 1695 they had fallen on hard times. However the rising confidence of the local farmers led to this new market being established for cattle and was to be held on the 1st Tuesday in January and the 15 May annually. The 1823 market reported brisk trading and good prices. On 1 January 1828 the usual market took place but the cattle were of inferior quality and sales were dull with many beasts unsold. By January 1830 the market was rapidly improving. It took place on the commonties around Thornhill and in this year four times the number of cattle were sold than the previous year. However the 1831 January market was very badly attended with only 48 cattle on show and sales were poor. Things recovered a little by January 1832 and cattle sales were much better. Nevertheless the market had moved to the second Tuesday in March by 1850. This roller coaster revue of the sales indicate that the Thornhill market was working at the margins of profitability and the May sales never really took off at all. Its long term viability was always in doubt, probably because of the massive nearby markets at Crieff and Falkirk.

Nevertheless local farm workers were proud of their skills and rarely missed an opportunity to display them. By March 1820 an annual ploughing competition had been instigated. The competition moved around the various farms of the district and no doubt few farmers objected to expert ploughing being done on their land in the name of competition. The 1820 competition took place at Moss Side owned by Mr. Paterson and it was reported that there were a vast number of spectators. In 8 February 1826 the ploughing match was organised in the name of 'Thornhill Farming Club' and took place this year at Ward of Goodie. Thirteen ploughs entered with the first prize going to James Johnston of Gartincaber. The Johnstons of Gartincaber were to dominate the ploughing competitions for some time.

A noticeable feature of almost all various gatherings throughout the nineteenth and early twentieth century was that they would be followed by a dinner and usually a dance with music as well. It is little wonder that we hear talk of the 'good old days' when we explore the social life of those who were comfortable in wealth. On this occasion the farming club dined, after the ploughing, in the Monteith Society Inn (now possibly Monteith House, 33 Main Street).

The annual ploughing competition has continued with only a few gaps almost up to the present day and the competition obviously helped to raise standards as an observer of the village noted in 1861:

'Thornhill stands second to none for well cultivated gardens and farms in the vicinity'.

A sample of entries from the competition gives us a picture of the scale of the event. On the 12 February 1869 it was at Munnieston. Twenty-eight ploughs competed with a large number of prize winners. Overall first was David Brown, servant to Robert McGowan of Ballinton. Fifth was Andrew Paterson, ploughman to our old friend Daniel MacFarlane, the Smith of Crosshill.

By 1884 there were two levels of competition, a junior and a senior. The senior ploughing competition was at Mr. Paterson's, McOrriston, and the junior one at Mr. Murdoch's, Boghall. There were 26 ploughs competing and it was a terrible day with stormy weather throughout. This did not deter a very large number of spectators from attending the event, or perhaps the attraction was more that the farmhouses were kept open for refreshments throughout the day. I imagine that an early draw was greatly sought after because the furrows would not be so straight after the traditional Thornhill hospitality!

The ploughing competitions would have presented a real challenge on the partially drained moss lands. Even as late as 1830 oxen on the moss were shod with broad pieces of wood to stop them from sinking. Moss improvements were still continuing apace in our area. In 1800 the Earl of Moray had built a 3 mile embankment from the dry field at Thornhill across the moss and over the Goodie Burn and by 1830 200 further acres of moss had been cleared around Thornhill.

Perhaps sinking into the moss was a farmer's fear that was now beginning to recede, but working with animals can always has its dangers. On the 11 July 1845 young Marjoribanks, the son of a local farmer, decided to help his father. He came to regret his helpfulness. He was leading a large calf to the Common by a rope. He rolled the rope around his waist and hit the calf with a stick to get it moving. Perhaps he was too enthusiastic with the stick because the calf took off and dragged him down the Main Street. Somehow the rope got tangled around his neck and it was reported that his scalp was laid bare!

He was very ill for some time but fortunately lived to tell the tale.

16. The 39 Steps of Local Families

By the 1830's it was noted that, as the houses improved and the average income gradually rose, there had been a big improvement in cleanliness and modes of living The community was pulling together more now as the moss farmers gradually became integrated. Indeed by 1840 Gaelic had almost completely died out as a spoken language here to be replaced by Scots. Amazingly however the last native Gaelic speaker in the district, looking back to his ancestry from the moss lairds, died as late as 1937.

In fact the descent of local families can be traced right up to the present day. One can only speculate upon what happened to the original 'moss lairds'. We know that many of them came from the Balquhidder area and shared a limited number of names, the most common being Stewart, Ferguson, MacLaren and McGregor.

The tracing of family trees can be a fascinating study. An early builder of houses in Thornhll was one Alexander Stewart. In 1797 he built the houses numbered 92 on the site of a stable and brewhouse (likely an illicit distillery at this time) and 79 Main Street on the site of waste ground. He also owned and possibly built the house called Slatehaa (once known as the slate hall).

It is interesting to speculate that Alexander, or his father, may well have been one of the original moss lairds who 'made good' and built their permanent dwellings in the growing village. There is strong evidence that this family can be traced into more recent times. It is likely that the same Alexander Stewart married Catherine Ferguson and had a daughter called Catherine. Catherine married a local man, descended from a family of small tenant farmers, called John Buchan and they later became publicans in Stirling. Their son, born at Drip in 1811, was also called John and became a lawyer and bank agent in Peebles. He was heavily involved in the City of Glasgow Bank failure of 1878 and he himself was an agent for the Commercial Bank. He had inherited the properties in Thornhill and fortunately was able to borrow money from the Commercial Bank using these properties as security. He thus saved himself from bankruptcy in the crash.

In spite of his financial difficulties he managed to think about other things as well and he and his wife (also called Catherine) had a number of children. One was to become the Rev. John Buchan, a free church minister. He, in 1875, had a son also called John and this son was to achieve great fame and fortune as the author of '39 Steps', 'Greenmantle' and other adventure tales. He was knighted for his efforts and was to become the first Lord Tweedsmuir!

There are still a number of Fergusons, McGregors, Stewarts, McCullochs, Patersons and McLarens in the village area and perhaps in some cases we may have living evidence of the early population growth of this part of West Perthshire.

The use of nicknames has been a tradition in many rural areas of Scotland and Thornhill is no exception. The origin of nicknames is the limited number of surnames found in one area combined with the tendency to use family names from one generation to another. In Thornhill we come across 'Duncan the Reiver', 'Ruskie Rab'(a publican in the Crown Hotel during the mid 18th century), 'Kippen Jock', 'Angus the Leer'(how did he get this name?) and many more. This tradition continues, to a limited extent, into the present day.

McLachlan

Fig. 20. The Main Street at Slatehaa 1904

The house to the front left was another property probably built by Alexander Stewart along with Slatehaa (the first slated house in the village) to the right. Note the Victorian widows dress worn by the lady to the right. At this time the pavements, the responsibility of the house occupants, were in a very poor state of repair on the North side of the Main Street.

17. The Early Water Supply

It is recorded in 1744 that Mr. Home Drummond, at his own expense, brought an excellent supply of spring water by pipes to the village. A storage tank was built to the west end of the North Common and a series of pumps were installed in the Main Street (e.g. Roseneath), and in the Low Town. It is claimed that Thornhill was one of the first settlements to enjoy piped water from one of the many wells and hydrants placed at intervals along the street and by the commons.

The iron pumps were notable for having lions' heads but alas they have now all disappeared. On the Main Street long arm pumps gave a source of water. Low Town residents were one up on their Main Street friends because the head of water was enough to allow them just to turn a handle for their fresh water. However there was no water supply installed in the houses themselves yet. They were to wait some time for this!

Prior to this supply most of the water supply came from wells. The most prominent line was to be found at the bottom of the gardens of houses on the South side of Main Street. Here, at least five wells adjoined the common land. Another major well was opposite 'pipers cottage'.

Inevitably these wells would have been the social centre of the village for the womenfolk, perhaps only matched by the washing area at the stream to the Western end of Low Town. This 18th century equivalent of the launderette was in a quarry by the Boquhapple Burn and provided a sheltered site for the washing. Fires were built in the base of the quarry and water was heated for the washing of the blankets and woollen goods. The bushes and trees round about were used as drying posts, but it was necessary to get there early on good washing days to make sure that enough space was left for the drying!

Fig.. 21 Main Street Thornhill 1904

McLachlan

This interesting photograph clearly shows the water pump just up the street from the Crown Hotel. Note also the single lamp outside the hotel. This was to serve as the sole village lighting for many years. The poor state of the pavements demonstrate that walking at night could be a hazardous affair.

18. The Tuneless Piper

Transport would not have been cheap. Residents had to pay for the upkeep of their local road and would use the toll roads (turnpikes) for travelling the longer distances. Most people would rarely leave their own parish boundary but for those who did the new road from Thornhill to the Bridge of Frew was a toll road, as was the road to Doune. Indeed the Toll House still stood at the road end opposite Burnside Cottage until it was demolished in 1935 and the Toll House at the Doune end of the road is still to be seen.

Fig. 22 Toll Road Cottage

This pleasant cottage was originally built to control access to the Thornhill - Doune road and would also take responsibility for the upkeep and maintenance of this road. Turnpike roads were a major step forward in opening up rural areas, but Thornhill remained relatively isolated throughout the 18th and 19th century.

Visitors, if they could afford the tolls, were welcomed into the Eastern approach to the village by the twin carvings of a piper and a drummer and these became well-known landmarks. They were constructed on an old arched entrance into the estate of Ballinton but were moved in the 1770's. They were later mounted on either side of the small bridge at the entrance to Thornhill. Alas vandalism was not unknown then and both statues were pushed off the bridge. The drummer was broken but the piper survived minus a left leg.

Fig. 23 Pipers Cottage

This old cottage once boasted of the Ballinton piper, who was mounted on the gable. Although the formal name of the house is no longer 'Pipers Cottage' it still bears this name locally. The piper is now gone now and was believed to have been taken away to the Abercairney Estates. If any reader can throw any light on the present whereabouts - can we have it back? (See Appendix 2)

Fig. 24 The Thornhill Piper

Stirling Observer

Thousands of visitors to Thornhill saw the figure of the piper at the entrance to the village. He is playing a curious mix of the Highland Pipe and the Lowland Pipe; the instrument being mouth blown but having two drones from a single stock.

19. Murder and Mystery

The level of recreation in a society is a useful measurement of its prosperity and it is noticeable that as the 18th century progressed the village society was becoming more homogenous and communal events and facilities grew rapidly. However we hear of the minister of the parish, John Sommers, (1810 - 1839) who led a campaign against cock fighting which was very popular in the village. This would have upset the schoolmaster who traditionally organised the betting at these events and found it a very useful addition to his salary. However the schoolmaster would have had mixed loyalties because he also doubled as the church session clerk!

Excitement, perhaps dampened by the minister's campaign, rose again on other occasions. Tradition tells us that in the early part of the 19th century there was a serious domestic argument between a man and wife in a house, which still stands, in Low Town. The altercation, believed to be over the wife's adultery, led to the woman running out into the garden and climbing to the top of a haystack. The man followed her and set fire to it, causing the woman to die of burns. There were no local police then but Baillies from Doune got to hear about it and travelled to Thornhill for a dramatic capture. They took the culprit to Doune where he was publicly shackled to the cross that was then outside the Balhaldie Inn. He relied on food from sympathetic locals and perhaps it was a relief when he was taken to Stirling and imprisoned in the Tollbooth. At his trial he could well be considered lucky to be sentenced to penal servitude spending the rest of his life in Australia. He fared better than a man called Scobie who was a nephew of James Scobie of Cessintully in 1807. Quite what the argument was about is not recorded, but a local feud with one of the sons of Mr. Murdoch of Gartincaber ended in his murder at Longridge and the execution of Scobie in Edinburgh.

This reminded people of a previous local scandal involving George McKerracher. He was accused of forgery and although widely believed to be innocent he was prosecuted and condemned to death. It is said that he was given an opportunity to escape when travelling from Perth Prison to Stirling but he said:

'I am innocent and not afraid to meet almighty god'

He was 'justified'(hanged) on the 28 April 1783 and along with Agnes Fisher he was buried in Norrieston Churchyard. (See Appendix 1)

Further outrage occurred when horses with broken harnesses from the regular mail coach to Aberfoyle appeared back in Thornhill shortly after passing through the village. A village possee set out to investigate and found the mail coach overturned at side of road by the Mollins, a short way along the Aberfoyle road. The coachman had been robbed and murdered. The murderer was never caught and the mystery remains to this day. However a postscript to the story is that sightings of a mysterious coachman in recognisable period dress have been reported in the area.

A local ghost?

Perhaps this apparition is well acquainted with the friendly spook said to be often busy behind 15 Main Street, or perhaps he prefers the phantom said to be continuing its activities at Hillview or the Spectre demonising a house in Low Town.

Part 3: The Victorian Era

20. The Demon Drink

The great public advances of the 18th century such as electoral reform and the health, housing and factory acts helped the everyday life of people to become a bit more pleasant. Thornhill reflected this by the mushrooming of activities and societies in the village and the public celebrations that became even more prevalent. The agricultural societies and the church had already built up a recreational role but these were soon followed by many more.

The celebrations for the new year have their origins deep in history but had certainly not been forgotten. The celebrations, that lasted for two days or more, were marked by a great deal of good humour and occasional boisterousness but very rarely was there any trouble of any sort. However there was an element of excessive drinking and many villagers felt deep concern at this.

Their response, in 1846, was to set up the 'Thornhill Total Abstinence Society'. Members agreed to pledge the following:

"I hereby promise to abstain from ale, porter, shrub, wine, ginger cordial and all other intoxicating liquors, except as medicines or in a religious ordinance. Furthermore that I will neither give nor offer them to others and that I will discontinue all the causes and practices of intemperance"

The first president was John MacFarlane and the treasurer was Thomas Stewart. The society proved to be very popular and was to exert a considerable influence on the village. One hundred and forty-four members signed the pledge between 29 August 1846 and 4 August 1847. The group met on the first Monday of every month and continued meeting until March 1933 under the new name of the Thornhill Gospel Temperance Society. They organised many social events including an annual soiree on 1 January annually.

We hear that in 1877 the soiree was very successful and the village was:

'animated throughout the day with some turbulent behaviour but no problems ensued and everybody was very good natured'

An associated society, in conjunction with the church, was the 'Band of Hope' Temperance Society, which began in 1883. It had weekly Friday meetings and the occasional social such as the large soiree on 19 February 1884 for all adult and junior temperance band members. The Band of Hope was very well supported and by 1910 had 70 regular members and was to continue well into the twentieth century.

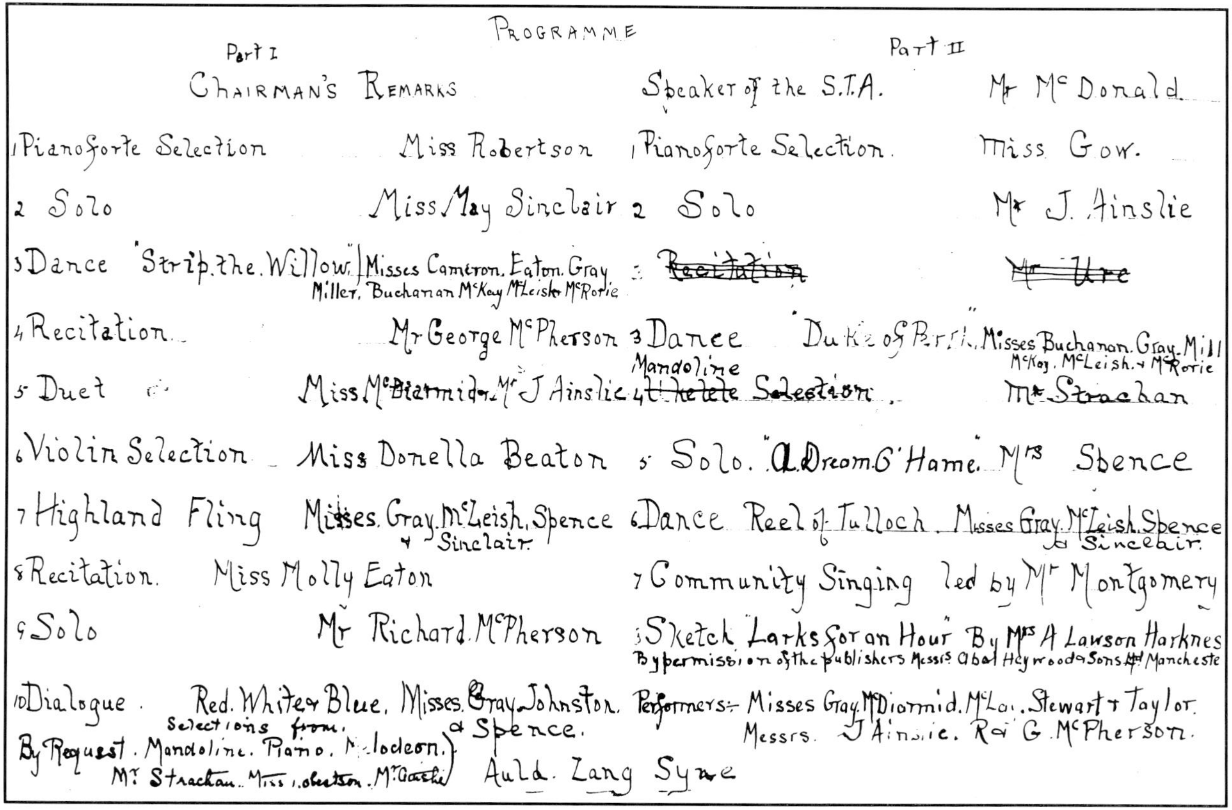

PROGRAMME

Part I		Part II	
Chairman's Remarks		Speaker of the S.T.A.	Mr McDonald
1 Pianoforte Selection	Miss Robertson	1 Pianoforte Selection.	Miss Gow.
2 Solo	Miss May Sinclair	2 Solo	Mr J. Ainslie
3 Dance "Strip the Willow"	Misses Cameron, Eaton, Gray, Miller, Buchanan, McKay, McLeish, McRorie	3 ~~Recitation~~	~~Mr Ure~~
4 Recitation	Mr George McPherson	3 Dance "Duke of Perth"	Misses Buchanan, Gray, Mill, McKay, McLeish & McRorie
5 Duet	Miss McDiarmid & Mr J Ainslie	4 Mandoline ~~Ukelele~~ Selection	Mr Strachan
6 Violin Selection	Miss Donella Beaton	5 Solo. "A Dream O' Hame."	Mrs Spence
7 Highland Fling	Misses Gray, McLeish, Spence & Sinclair	6 Dance Reel of Tulloch	Misses Gray, McLeish, Spence & Sinclair.
8 Recitation.	Miss Molly Eaton	7 Community Singing	led by Mr Montgomery
9 Solo	Mr Richard McPherson	8 Sketch "Larks for an Hour" By Mrs A Lawson Harknes	By permission of the publishers Messrs Abel Heywood & Sons Ltd Manchester
10 Dialogue. Red. White & Blue.	Misses Gray, Johnston, & Spence.	Performers:- Misses Gray, McDiarmid, McLa.., Stewart & Taylor. Messrs. J Ainslie. Ra.. G. McPherson.	
By Request. Selections from Mandoline. Piano. Melodeon.	Mr Strachan. Miss Robertson. Mr Gaelic	Auld Lang Syne	

Spence

Fig. 25 Entertainment temperance style.

This temperance concert programme of 1927 was hand written and must have involved a huge time commitment for the writers. Note the large and varied programme. If a mistake occurred then the offending word was crossed out rather than re-writing all the programmes. Note that almost all the entertainers were local people.

21 Fun and Games

An important day in the social calendar was Auld Hansel Monday, which was the third Monday in January. On 18 January 1858 a new venture held on the South Common burst onto the scene. It was called the Thornhill Gymnastic Games. In fact we would recognise these as the modern Highland Games. This first one had Deanston Brass Band plus an unnamed Pipe Band leading a street parade (which finished up at Sorley's Inn), and the games themselves had all the components of the modern Highland Games, such as highland dancing (fling, swords, etc.), putting the stone, throwing the hammer, tossing the caber (William Ferguson of Lanrick was the first winner), and athletics competitions including races for local men and boys. There were a large number of spectators and it is heartening to report that in an age when we usually hear of factories paying little attention to their workers, the Deanston Adelphi Cotton Mill (a very large employer in the area) was closed for the afternoon. In the evening came the Thornhill Ball, held in the school. This was very successful and was attended by 60 couples. An eyewitness account said:

> *"The lassies looked very bonnie, whose gay dresses and blooming faces added not a little to the pleasure of the evening. Cupid was plying his darts freely."*

For a time the Gymnastic games continued to flourish. On 24 January 1862 the 5th annual Thornhill Games were held. By this time there was a high standard of competition and the games were attracting people from a very wide area. As usual there was a procession after the Games to the Crown Hotel (This is the first recorded mention of the name of this hostelry) and then on to Sorleys Inn. By this time the Sorleys had built up a formidable and wide reaching reputation for their meals and it is encouraging to think that both the present day Lion and Unicorn and the Crown Hotel continue to provide first rate catering services. The dinner at Sorleys was excellent as usual and was followed by innumerable speeches. There seemed to be quite a talent in the village for after-dinner speaking. On this occasion we hear of Mr. MacLaren of Netherton having the guests rolling in the aisles with great a comedy rendition of a traditional highland sermon. The Gymnastic Games continued to grow and by 1865 the games had become a huge success as indeed was the ball in the evening. An immense crowd of villagers and visitors attended the events.

Regretfully over the next few years something led to the demise of the games. By 1878 they had been abandoned and the ball was now held during the new year celebrations to tie in with a fair held at west end of village. However the athletic tradition was upheld by Thornhill's John Ferguson who, on 22 August 1884, took part in a competition held at the West Lancashire Athletic Ground and won the half mile race in 1 minute 58.75 seconds, a creditable time even today.

We live in an age where our recreation is 'on tap' and we must admire the people of Thornhill for their enterprise in organising and running social and educational ventures of their own. The list of societies is very impressive and equally impressive is the tremendous support that most of the societies enjoyed.

The thriving music club held large annual concerts and dances throughout the century and well into the present one. Frequent intermediate concerts were also held. The music was mainly classical and local singers were always prominent. Scottish songs held a universal appeal, but never let it be said that the village was parochial. In May 1867, no doubt inspired by the events of the American Civil War, a group of local youths formed the 'Thornhill Negro Troupe' to sing Negro songs.

And very good they were too.

The young people of the village also formed a Flute Band. Indeed there was almost too much music, as a *'grand concert and nicht of Burns'*, held in February 1886, had for Thornhill a poor attendance and the reason given was:

'a plethora of social events in village'.

Yet activities were to intensify in the following year, for this was the Golden Jubilee celebration for Queen Victoria. National self confidence was high, the Empire was near its greatest extent and local patriotism certainly reflected this.

Colonel Drummond treated all the village children to tea, games, etc. at Blair Drummond House and almost all the village was decorated with flags:

'hardly a house in village without some mark of loyalty'.

On the celebratory day itself there was a national holiday. Pipers led a march of the local volunteers through the village and services were conducted in both the Established and the UF Kirk. This was followed by games on the South Common rather similar to the now defunct Gymnastic Games. Banquets in both the Commercial and the Crown Hotels were given by Lord Drummond for villagers, to be followed by a huge bonfire and fireworks on the common. The party was to last throughout the night!

Sporting societies also sprang up and by 1865 the Curling Club, using the 'Lug' on the North Common, had become well established. They competed against local clubs and also held a keenly fought internal annual competition. The first one was probably on 3 December 1869 with a prize of 3 pairs of curling stanes for the winners. In this year prize winners were:

1. Peter Ferguson
2. Robert Millar
3. Messrs. Sands, Duncanson, McLaren, Murray (Peter) and Murray (John) all equal.

The football club is a popular aspect of the village today with both Senior and Under 16 teams representing the village in the Forth and Endrick league. It is likely that the football club began in 1877. In June of that year the club played on a field at Netherton Farm and won 2-1 against Stirling Kings Park. What is astonishing is that there were among 300 and 400 spectators present! The team (called Vale of Menteith) played Doune in 1879 and were represented by

		Black		
	Duncanson	Jenkins		
	McGowan	Forrester	Dow	
McLaren	Ferguson	Irvine	Dickie	Fyfe

These august gentlemen may not wish to be remembered as on this occasion they lost 1 - 0. Perhaps this is the reason why in 1880 the football club held a New Year's Dance ....as a temperance ball!

Fig. 26 Curling Hut

This small brick hut overlooking the Lug once served as the storage area for the thriving curling club.

Fig. 27 The 'Lug'

Although little to see in this photograph it does illustrate the wild nature of the area which was once flooded and used as a curling pond.

Cricket also made an appearance. In July 1907 Thornhill Cricket Club was in existence playing on a field at Boquhapple and we hear of their triumph against Doune, a match which they won by 67 runs to 17.

In August 1877 a quoits club had been formed and played their first match against Doune. This club was to see intense but friendly rivalry against local teams for many years.

There was even more demand for sport. On 16 October 1908 a public meeting was called to organise and develop a Bowling Green and bowling on the new green by the Commercial Hotel remains a popular sport to the present day.

The golf lobby was not to be outdone. In September 1910 plans were drawn up for a golf course on Skeoch Brae on land kindly given by James Forrester. On 20 April 1911 the new golf course opened at Macrieston. There was a beautifully decorated arch at the entrance and the opening ceremony was grand. However the weather, which was terrible, was to prove a bad omen. Because of lack of funds the lease on the golf course was only to run for two years and sadly, in 1914, the golf club wound up with assets being given to Stirling Royal Infirmary

Shooting was a popular diversion and the annual shooting competition was keenly anticipated. The first was held on 1 January 1881, on this occasion organised by Daniel MacFarlane the Smith of Crosshill. The whole area had been noted in the New Statistical Account as being rich in wildlife, especially birds of prey. In the 1880's an excited commentator noted that:

> *'two horned or eared owls had been spotted at mid day on the Carse south west of Thornhill'.*

A nature lover?

He goes on to say proudly that both were shot and stuffed.

The common use of pigeons was for target practice on the moor but early tradition gives them another function. An example of this was recorded late in the last century. The Moss of Boquhapple was a favourite site for adders. A man was bitten and a Mr. John Marshall was sent to find a live pigeon. The unfortunate bird was torn to pieces and the warm flesh applied to the wound to extract venom:

> *'The flesh of the gentle dove is totally antagonistic to the poisonous venom of the vipers brood'.*

It is nice to report that the man recovered speedily and splendidly.

Glass ball shooting also gained prominence in the area and in 1888 a very cryptic message (probably aimed at the minister) appeared in the local press:

'warning to Thornhill sportsmen'

'The crack glass ball shots of Thornhill should keep a sharp lookout at present, as the 'black hen' with the short feathers is to be seen daily crackling loudly round the village'.

22. Draughts and the Devil

Activities of the mind were not neglected. One could argue whether draughts is a sport or a mental exercise but nevertheless the Thornhill Draughts team, established in the 1880's, distinguished themselves in competition until the outbreak of World War One.

Lectures were a consistent feature of the village. Every Monday evening was a 'penny lecture' involving a huge range of topics. The Thornhill section of the Young Men's Christian Association was active in this arena and by 1888 had formed a special literary association. A typical example of the time was in the week beginning 27 April 1888 when the literacy association of the local branch of the YMCA had a lecture on the 'French Revolution: its causes and effects.' Two days later came a public lecture entitled 'The Barometer and Weather'. Both were very well attended.

The thirst for knowledge and self improvement was strong indeed. The school organised continuation classes for senior pupils and those who had recently left school, on a purely voluntary basis and they proved to be very popular. In 1913 there were 17 students with average age of 13.5 years. Along with the adults of the village, they no doubt made good use of the library. There were no public or travelling libraries at this time and so, in 1892, Thornhill organised its own. It was held in the school and was open on Monday evening. The annual subscription for use was one shilling. This money, together with donations, was used to stock the shelves.

Communal events also increased and in particular we find that there were some events aimed specifically at the children of the village. In 1880 a picnic party, to become annual, was held for children and 140 attended. It began with a parade through the town followed by transport to the Lake of Menteith for the party itself. There were also the frequent journeys through the North Common and up Nellies Glen to the Skeoch Area for picnics. Apart from the fine views and pleasant surroundings the children would have been reminded and perhaps slightly frightened by the history around them. They would just see the edge of the field belonging to Hillhead Farm called the "guidane'. Our forefathers were nothing if not polite and this was one of the many cautious nicknames given to the devil himself. It was customary in this area to dedicate a field to 'the dark one' to keep him quiet. Hillhead was taking no chances as they had two 'guidanes'! Perhaps Hillhead was just too close to Nellies Glen for comfort. There is dispute concerning the Nellie who gave her name to the glen. Some say she was a serving girl from the Commercial Hotel who fell out of an upper window when watching a shooting party in the glen. A more accepted origin is from a lady called Nellie Christie. Nellie had a house on the park by the Commercial Hotel and was known by all around to be a witch. She must have been one of the non malicious variety as she lived to a good age.

Not all local witches were so harmless. John Miller (a Ruskie Miller) was puzzled by the unexplained continual loss of cattle. He decided that dark forces were to blame and said:

'They were witched, but I did for the blasted witch in the long run'

He cut the heart out of one of his dead beasts and stuck it full of nails, pins, and needles and put it in his peat stack. The heart disappeared after a time and the witch never bothered him again!

23. Education

The primary school in Low Town continues to enjoy a good reputation as it always has, with older residents often looking back fondly (and at times with some trepidation) at the strict but fair teachers who guided their early years. The present school was modernised and extended in 1873 to cater for the extra pupils as the Easter School had now closed down. The house now called 2 Low Town had become a residence but its link with the school children remained for some years as it became occupied by a lady who made toffee and was therefore very popular with the youngsters.

The now defunct Easter School was on the site of the present car park behind the Post Office. It was built about the beginning of 1800's as a place of worship for the 'new licht' anti-burghers and at the same time was used as a school. In 1820 the hall was purchased solely as a school following the uniting of burghers and anti burghers with the congregation of the Bridge of Teith Church. The school was called the Grammar School, but was usually known as the Easter School and was non denominational. It became the Village Hall following the changes resulting from the Education Act of 1872.

Generally the reputation of the school ensured a good supply of first rate teachers but there seemed to be a problem in the middle of the 18th century. In 1845 a series of adverts appeared seeking a teacher, despite there being 80 pupils at school. Internal difficulties reigned, but we do not know what these problems were. However they did not last too long and soon the school was back to normal and began to tick off its achievements. Training firemen is not one of the usual ones, but in December 1902 the boys at the school were financially rewarded for putting out a serious fire! Academic achievement has been noticeable too. James McLaren was born at Middleton in 1853 from a long standing local family and he quickly shone at school. He ultimately became an architect and his first professional project was to design a new wing for the Stirling High School. He became a leading light in the emerging Arts and Crafts movement and fulfilled a number of important contracts in London and the South of England. A promising young Glasgow designer was said to have been considerably influenced by James - his name was Charles Rennie MacIntosh! McLaren's greatest achievement was the design of the unique planned village of Fortingall shortly before his tragically early death from tuberculosis in 1890.

1964 was a good year for the school because 6 of the former P1 class graduated with degrees or higher diplomas. They were Ian Black, Jean Paterson, David Stewart, Kathleen Ferguson, David Thomson and Lorna Hutton, a fine record for a small village school (see Appendix 6).

24. Discipline and the Church

Feelings had begun to run high about the now very dilapidated Chapel of Ease and the astronomic cost for its repair and gradually plans consolidated for a new church. The present Norriston Church was the result being opened in 1879. It is an admirable building designed in the 'Early English' ecclesiastical style, with a fine 90 foot high tower. It is now a listed building.

The old Chapel of Ease was demolished but the bell was saved as it was believed to have special properties. In the 18th century it was said that a woman called Mary Brown could tell by toll of the Norrieston Bell when there was going to be a funeral. She was kept busy because another common superstition in Norrieston was that deaths occurred in threes.

Strong feelings had also been expressed about the established church itself for some time. Protest about the attempts of King Charles I to introduce 'English' Episcopalian characteristics into the church, such as bishops and a new prayer book, brought massive popular protest in many parts of Scotland. This led to the first mass petition called 'the Covenant'. Supporters were called 'covenanters'

This was a 'covenanting' district.

In the late 17th century an early Norrie (an ancestor of who you will remember gave us the land and name Norrieston) tried to rescue an ousted minister and supporter of the covenant from arrest, but he was brutally killed by soldiers somewhere in Moss below Boquhapple. No doubt this hardened the strong religious beliefs of the district and in the 18th Century numerous religious sects grew up to fight the established church. The village founder, Archibald Napier, would not have endeared himself locally either. It was said (Ramsay of Ochtertyre) that Napier's:

"ideas were very much English".

Thornhill embraced the religious controversy with enthusiasm and in the 1780's a third of the population of Kincardine Parish were seceders of various kinds; a very high local percentage.

The religious controversy continued into the 19th century and led ultimately to the disruption of 1843, in which a large section of the Church of Scotland seceded and set up the Free Church. The United Free Church was built next to the Norrieston Parish Church and ran in competition for many years.

Fig. 28 The Parish Church of Norrieston.

This photograph, taken almost 100 years age, looks remarkably like the present day view, and is a tribute to the conservation of this area. The church, built in 1879, is in the Early English style and is now a listed building. The manse and UF church can be seen in the background.

The two churches were to exert a powerful influence on the everyday life of the village, tending to concentrate upon the social and moral welfare of the community as well as the spiritual side. Prior to the establishment of the Norrieston Parish in 1878 much of the business was done by the Kincardine Parish Church. Discipline was very strict. A transgressor was dressed in a sackcloth and was forced to sit on a black stool (stool of repentance) underneath a board saying 'place of repentance'. The shame for a proud people would have been near unbearable. Discipline was to remain strict for some time.

Kirk session records of the 18th century are dominated by the investigation of the moral rectitude of the parish. For example on 1 November 1858 James Lawson and his wife Margaret McKerracher applied to be brought under church discipline for:

'antenuptial fornication'.

They had to appear before the kirk session to explain their case. It is good to know that they were absolved from scandal at the next meeting. There were very many similar cases throughout the century.

In 1862 a young girl was:

'purged from the scandal of fornication'.

One wonders what a torture it must have been for these young people to appear before a room full of the church elders to explain their position. It would have been particularly upsetting for the number of unmarried mothers who had to explain themselves. It is noticeable that usually it was the girl who bore the brunt and the father often escaped unscathed.

It is easy to come to the conclusion that Thornhill was a hot bed of 'sin' but in fact the village was no worse than any other. Kirk Session records throughout Scotland show a similar picture. What is heartening locally was the attitude of the elders, who almost without exception gave forgiveness and welcomed the miscreants back into the fold, often giving them considerable support. The leaders of the community were well recognised for their services. One such was James McLaren of Middleton who, in 1859, was presented with an inscribed gold watch for:

'his reforming zeal and strength as servant and master, temperance and the moral elevation of community'.

Fig. 29 The UF Church

Following the serious disruptions within the Church of Scotland in 1843 a new Free Church was formed taking a large number of ministers with it. In Thornhill there was considerable support for the new church, and the United Free Church above was built to serve the new demands. It was to remain a separate church until 1927 and was later converted into the Church Hall.

On the spiritual side the strength of the two congregations was impressive. There were huge attendances at the weekly services and both kirks had very active choirs and Sunday schools. There was a regular series of socials, dances and picnics such as the very successful annual picnic, which went far and wide. In 1907 it visited Arran; quite a feat considering the transport available at this time.

A major role of the church was the care of the poor. Initially Kincardine dealt with Thornhill cases. For example in 1728 we can read that:

'Malise Graham to get winter fyre to family'.

'To a dead coffin to Patrick McArthur his wife in Norrieston £3 Scots'.

Cases of genuine need were sympathetically treated but short shrift was given to those who were suspected of insincerity. An officer was appointed, called locally 'buff the beggar' to drive off what he considered the vagrant class of the community. The Buff was not always gentle as they were also called 'baton men'. Mr. Sands from Thornhill, a well known local figure, served for some time as a baton man in the late 19th century.

The fund for the relief of the genuine poor was the Mort Cloth Society and the community were encouraged to keep up their Mort Cloth dues. The welfare state of the mid 20th century finally brought an end to this rather hit or miss method of poor relief.

The Ministers themselves who made such an impact upon this community have been well documented in William King's publication 'Norrieston Church'. However mention must be made of the remarkable Reverend George Williams. He was minister of the UF church for over forty years straddling this century and was to make his mark in many ways. He was described as a man of wide information and power of research and many old tales would have been lost had he not meticulously recorded them. He was an archaeologist and antiquary and his name has been numbered amongst the leading minor poets of Scotland. He also had scientific leanings and was an authority in botany. His publications are many and varied from 'Scottish Psalms in Metre' to the 'History of Coinage'. He also had a sense of humour as he showed when describing one of his predecessors, the Reverend Patrick Caldwell (1775 - 1796).

Caldwell was notorious for his difficult wife. One day he was the visiting preacher at Gargunnock, but clearly his mind was not completely on the job in hand. Throughout the service he continually looked nervously back towards Thornhill. When asked why he explained that it was:

"In case my wife sets fire to the manse".

At a later service in Norrieston he thought that Mr. Lennox had fallen asleep during his sermon. He shouted:

"waken that cauper there".

Unperturbed Lennox replied:

"the caupers no sleepin sir, jist ye stick to the point"

Freemasonry was prominent in the village and in the early days the connection with the church, especially the Free Church, was very strong and many Masonic Lodge services were conducted in the UF church. The only alternative was for the freemasons to make their way to neighbouring villages where a lodge was in existence and in the days of difficult transport it illustrates their commitment. The nearest lodges were at Doune and Callander and local masons were prominent in both. The Rev. George Williams was to be a leading light in developing the lodge in Thornhill and he organised a committee which approached Colonel Drummond, himself an enthusiastic mason, for a plot of land. The Colonel approved of the idea and made land at the cross-roads available. George Crabbie (of Green Ginger fame) owned the nearby Blairhoyle Estate and he agreed to build a hall at his own expense on the site gifted by Colonel Drummond. The Lodge Charter was granted on 2 February 1893 and the official opening of the Lodge Blairhoyle No. 792, preceded by a procession through the village, took place on Saturday 21 October 1893. The superb new facility gave an increased profile to the Lodge in the village and inductions were frequent and well publicised over the next few years.

The building itself, reputably the smallest purpose built lodge in Scotland, is a listed red sandstone building with a tower affording commanding views, topped by an interesting weather vane at its apex. It was built in the 'arts and craft' movement style and was widely admired. It still is, acting as a source of interest and a landmark to travellers passing through the village (see cover photograph)

Thornhill was also one of the first places in Scotland where the union of the established kirk and free kirk took place in 1927, which was two years before the official union of the churches. The United Free Church Manse was sold in 1932. With the proceeds the United Free Kirk itself, after a period of disagreement, was finally converted in 1937 into the Church Hall, a function that continues today.

25. Markets and Fairs.

By 1850 the cattle market was struggling to continue and in an attempt to breathe life into it the timings were moved to the second Tuesday in March. By 1851 there were over 200 cattle and horses in attendance. However over the years the market had gradually mutated into an agricultural show and in future years this show element was to become prominent although occasional cattle sales continued throughout the century on the traditional dates. The first formal agricultural show began in July 1851. The pattern quickly became established as competitions developed across the whole range of farm animals, and there were of the order of thirty separate classes to be competed for. It gives a reflection of the times that many of the competitions were aimed specifically at feuars in the village. It indicated that to keep a pig, poultry, a horse and a few cows was the norm for the village residents and the Commons would have been heavily used for grazing their stock. The show, as with most village events, quickly became a major social occasion and was always followed by dinner and speeches, usually at Sorleys (now the Lion and Unicorn) or Hay's (probably now the Crown). The tenth annual show took place on the 24 July 1860. It was held on the park adjoining Sorleys Inn (this would be by the North Common). For the first time some judging was held indoors in Mr. Sorleys new hall, which he wanted to show off as he had had it fitted out just for the purpose.

Occasional grain sales also took place. This is an old tradition and Robert Burns writes graphically at the incredible scenes of drunkenness that usually accompanied these events. It is unlikely that Thornhill was an exception. On 23 August 1851 grain sales took place at three farms. The local tradition was to have a free and ample supply of whisky at such country sales but it is reported that at this one drunkenness was not as bad as it used to be.

Perhaps this indicated a new business approach to farming. The old communal approach, often a social occasion in itself, seemed to be dying. It was noted on 23 September 1859 that the custom of 'kirns' at end of the harvest had almost disappeared:

> *'The old farmers have been succeeded by a new class who practise rigid economy with their workers. Instead of 'gude kail and beef diners' there is now an apology for a dinner, often made up only of bread and milk'.*

Not everybody supported the new economies and a certain local worthy miller was determined to keep up the old local customs. He had a 'rantin a' kirn':

'30 -40 hale and hearty lads as ever wielded a scythe, and blooming lasses as ever lifted a sheaf came to give the miller a days work. Grain fell fast before the scythe and was quickly sheafed by the nimble fingered lifters. By the time the sun was going down the miller's entire cutting for the year was finished.

The whole party then went to his house and had a good substantial supper. Then the room was cleared for a dance which went on with great spirit until the early hours. The miller thanked them all profusely for their work, and they thanked him in return saying that a helping hand would not be awanting on their part the next time they had like work to do'.

These new 'economic' farmers saw a gradual rise in prosperity through the years of the 19th century. Even the terrible potato blight, which was to cause so much hardship and famine in the late 1840's and early 1850's in Ireland and the Highlands, had a minimum impact on the area, although there were frequent rather panic reports as late as 1858 about 'disease in potatoes again'.

The majority of local people would still have earned their livelihood on the land, either as farm workers or small tenant farmers. Life for them had not changed much despite the rapid changes in agriculture in the late 17th and early 18th century. This was because most of the surrounding lands were still sizeable estates owned by gentlemen farmers. The business of running and farming the land was usually left to the Factor and the Grieve.

There was also the droving trade. A number of people who were local or who were to settle in the village area were employed in the droving of cattle from the Highlands to local markets. This important trade lasted well over two hundred years and was to continue until after World War One. The fathers of at least two present residents were engaged in this trade. They would be away from home for months at a time as they walked from Lochaber and other such areas, often sleeping with the cattle by night.

The life of the farm workers was usually equally basic. They often had a nomadic existence tending to take contracts from the farmers for six months only and then often moving on. They may have been asked to stay if they were liked but often they would move to the highest bidder - a necessity when farm worker's wages were notoriously low, even in an age when overall wages generally were depressed. It is recorded that a well-respected worker left his employment and moved to the Lanrick Estate at the end of the last century. The offer for him, astonishing in our age of the massive soccer transfer fee, was one penny more a week!

By 1860 the farming communities were examining ways to streamline and improve the hiring of workers. On the 6 July of this year a public meeting was held to discuss the possibility of an annual 'feeing' fair, to be held at the Cross (the cross-roads) to hire harvest workers. It was agreed that this would be on the 2nd Tuesday of July annually. The first fair was a great success with many workers gaining new employment. The average wages were for men from £3 10 shillings to £4, and for women from £2 - £2 7 shillings.

No equal rights at this time!

In Thornhills' now accustomed style the same evening as the first 'feeing' fair was the 'Doune Gardeners Lodge' procession followed by a concert of local talent. A great attraction was always the local favourite, Mr Robert Forrester, who excelled in telling monologues.

The feeing fair and the accompanying period of time for the farm workers known as the 'flitting' was to last well into the twentieth century. Of course the 'feeing fair' was an excellent excuse for a get together and the route from the fair back to their farms was often fairly long and tortuous after a long evening's 'rest and relaxation'.

The ploughmen and young farmers saw no reason why they should not get an opportunity for a break even if they were not involved in the 'flitting.' Hence the tradition of the ploughman's picnic and the young farmer's excursion was born. The Ball and the excursions became annual. For example in 1883 the young farmers had an excursion to Tarbet and Arrochar with the Ploughman's Ball the following night. Forty couples attended and the dance lasted until 0500 am. The girls attracted a great deal of attention and after much deliberation the:

> *'girl with the brown velvet dress tied with the girl from Doune as 'Belle of the Ball''*

By 1887 the Ploughman's Annual Picnic had become a highlight of the year for the young folk. In that year James Stewart erected a fine decorative arch right across the Main Street outside the Crown Hotel. Then a whole series of horses and decorated cars (provided by W. McLaren of Drumore, J. Paterson of Stock o' Broom, J. McLaren of Middleton, P. Mailer of Mosside and Mr. D. Stewart) were made available to carry the 60 young farmers to Loch Ard and Aberfoyle.

West End, Thornhill.

Fig. 30 Thornhill West End looking towards the Cross-roads Circa 1910

McLachlan

A group of bemused well dressed children look at the photographer. The scene today is not too dissimilar but Hillview on the corner has changed and the house to the foreground of the cross-roads has been demolished. There is, of course, no war memorial

26. The Great and Good

It was not all play and no work! Life for farm workers was very hard and strict and summary dismissal was always possible. A local resident tells of Burnbank Farm, owned by Mr Paterson. He was a gentlemen farmer and the practical running of the estate was done by his Grieve. One morning Mr. Paterson, hurrying to an engagement in Stirling took half a pie from the pantry cupboard to see him on his way. When he returned the house was in uproar with the maid sacked and in tears as she had been accused of stealing the pie. Mr. Paterson sheepishly had to admit to taking his own pie!

The maid was reinstated.

Not all the employers were mean and uncaring. A local worker was carrying coal in his horse and cart to Lanrick a few years after the coming of the Doune - Callander railway. The horse, unaccustomed to trains, took fright and reared when one passed by. The unfortunate worker was thrown off the cart and crushed under the ringed iron wheels of the cart. At least his unfortunate widow was looked after by the estate, being given a small pension and work at Lanrick.

However the history of Thornhill is not the history of the great landowners and statesmen. It is the history of the everyday life of a Scottish community with little time for rank and pretension. This was well summed up by Archibald MacDonald (grandfather of a present resident) towards the end of the last century. He met a duchess with associated retinue on a narrow bridge and was told to move. He refused:

"Do you know who I am"?

asked the frustrated duchess, and Archibald knew fine:

"Yes, but I don't care if you are the duchess from hell. I was on the brig afore you. You move"!

I understand that she did.

It would be wrong to suppose that the folk of Thornhill had an antipathy to the large landowner. The Lanrick estate has already shown that care of their tenants and workers was not ignored.

Lanrick was relatively much closer to Thornhill, in terms of ease of access, than it is today. There was a direct route from Thornhill North to the Lanrick Ford as can be seen on William Johnson's map of 1827 (fig 16) and many local people worked on the estate. The house of Lanrick stands on the site of a very early settlement, probably a tower house, but it was 'gothicised' with turrets and battlements in 1791.

The interior at this time was particularly grand, although some thought rather ostentatious:

'more magnificent than convenient'
(Ramsay of Ochtertyre 1801)

Sands / Diggens

Fig. 31   Lanrick Castle in the 19th century

Landrick is not considered to be particularly close to Thornhill today, but until this century it was connected with Thornhill by hill routes and rights of way. An early drove route and a major route from the North used the ford at Lanrick, went onto Thornhill and then travelled via the Bridge of Goody onto the major crossing point of the Forth at Frew. This strategic position at the Highland margin and the Teith crossing has helped the house to develop a rich history, especially with its strong Jacobite connections. Sadly it is now in a ruinous condition.

At the time of the 1745 rebellion the estate was under the control of the Haldane family, and they raised a troop of horse to serve the Prince in his abortive campaign. Later the house passed to the Macgregors, who had also loyally supported the Jacobite cause.

The MacGregor owners had obviously reached better times by the early 19th century and the house was known as Clan Gregor Castle and the impressive but not well known MacGregor Monument was built in the grounds. Sir Euan Murray Macgregor later sold Lanrick to Mr. William Jardine MP, a well-known Dumfriesshire Laird. Jardine had made his name for his business activities with James Matheson in the far east. They built their fortune from the Opium trade but their partnership ultimately spread to more legitimate and acceptable activities. As Jardine Matheson, their firm grew into one of the largest

84

trading concerns in the world. The house of Lanrick is today little more than an empty shell with only distant echoes of its illustrious past disturbing the peace of the riverside location.

The Home Drummond's of Blair Drummond often exercised a paternalistic overview of the village despite their controversial claims to common ground in the Moss. In 1840 there was a large party in Thornhill to celebrate the marriage of Mr Home - Drummond younger. Eighty people attended a banquet at Lambs Inn and there were over 25 speeches following the meal. The initial water supply to the village was also courtesy of the Drummonds and when the system was improved in 1836 this was a present from the laird to the village to celebrate the coming of age of his son. Cynics say that the water supply was needed to quench the thirst of the village following his 21st birthday party!

Just three years later in May 1859 the 'new' school was being built in Low Town courtesy of Lord Home Drummond and with a little alteration and improvement is still serving its purpose well today.

It does appear that the Home Drummonds were well liked. On 26 August 1830 the village held a celebration for Lord Home Drummond on the occasion of his re-election as the local Member of Parliament. They were not the only ones to celebrate because even the prisoners in Stirling Gaol sent a congratulatory address to him. Perhaps the prisoners had an ulterior motive because he responded by giving them all a very good dinner!

There are numerous buildings in the village associated with the Drummond family. Norrieston House on the Main Street, a listed building dating from the early 18th century was by repute the tied house of the Factor of the Drummond Estates. As a result there would be a nominal rent payable and as late as this century the rent was said to be:

'one red rose annually'

This was probably the rent paid by Sandy Macarthur, who died here in 1921 having spent 81 years working on the Blairdrummond Estate. He only retired in 1920 from his active duties as overseer when the Thornhill portion of the estate was sold in that year.

Benview, situated on The Hill, dates from at least 1769 and probably earlier. The tack on the property was granted by Agatha Drummond probably to her gamekeeper. At a later date the house seemed to be used as a temporary manse, in all likelihood for the Chapel of Ease. As a consequence, possibly because of Thornhill's reputation at this time, it was put in the deeds that occupiers were not allowed to:

'sell ale and spirits on the premises'!

Like almost all the other old feus in the village a glimpse into a lifestyle now past is given by the clauses in the deeds that allow the use of the surrounding commonties for the:

'cutting of turf (probably for thatch), the grazing of animals and the use of the quarry for stone'.

Fig. 32
Benview

Dating from the early 18th century this house may well have served as an early manse, and probably was the home of divinity students, once plentiful in Thornhill.

Fig. 33
Norrieston House

Situated in Norrieston close to the original Chapel of Ease these listed houses may be the oldest in the village, dating from at least 1757. By repute this building was the traditional home of the Factor of giant Drummond Estate

Fig 34. Blair Drummond

Blair Drummond House was the home of the Home Drummonds. From the time of Lord Kames and his ambitious drainage schemes the Drummond family played a significant role in the growth of Thornhill, especially in the development of the water supply and the school buildings. This photograph was taken circa 1900 and shows the 'new house' of 1868 which replaced the older one designed by the Earl of Mar, a well known architect (and leader of the Jacobite Army of 1715 in his spare time).

27. Devils, Bears and the Crimean War

A memorable event occurred at Ballinton, the ancient home of the Napiers, on 4 June 1886 and illustrates once again that Thornhill was not backward in coming forward if there was a good party to be had. George McGowan, the owner, held a grand ball. There was a large dance floor cleared in the granary and at least 26 different dances, often repeated, took place accompanied by songs and various dancing demonstrations. At 4 am things were beginning to wind down but no agreement could be made about who was the Belle of the Ball. However Miss Agnes Stevenson and Miss Maggie Richardson were voted the best dancers much to their delight. When it was time to go home Mr and Mrs McGowan shook each person's hand before they departed, to the rings of 'for he's a jolly good fellow'. A report of the time said:

> *'So ended one of the best affairs at Ballinton since the Napiers, when the 'de'il himself in the guise of a big black dog, jumped out of one of the high windows of Ballinton following an interview with the Napier laird who had vigorously refused the terms of the contract proposed by his satanic majesty'.*

The house of Gartincaber also provides local interest. The Burn-Murdochs occupied the estate for much of the 19th century and well into the present century and took an active interest in village affairs. The Burn-Murdoch's traced their descent from Murdoch of Cumloch, a leading follower of Robert Bruce. The early part of this listed house dates from the late 1400's - early 1500's but most of it was built in the 1760's and in 1843. An article in the Scottish Gardener of December 1910 describes the impressive garden and trees such as the grove of lime trees planted in 1747. It also noted that on prominent display near the house was a bell and cannon ball from Sevastopol brought home during the Crimean War. A prominent landmark nearby is Gartincaber Tower built in 1790. No-one is sure of the exact function of this folly but it is often said that it was to mark the geographical centre of Scotland. Clearly the builder was not a Geographer!

Fig. 35 Gartincaber at the Turn of the Century

This fine house has an ancient origin and the wing to the left of the photograph is mainly 18th century in origin. The wing to the right is Victorian. The estate was once renowned for its gardens and some of its many glasshouses are shown to the right of the house. The impressive avenue of lime trees is behind the house. This photograph dates from circa 1910 but the house has not withstood the rigours of the twentieth century unscathed. Fortunately it is now in the process of restoration.

Fig. 36 Gartincaber Tower : the centre of Scotland?

Perhaps a better geographer would have been a certain resident of Braendam. This was our own local empire builder who, had he kept a diary, would have told a fascinating story of the early attempts of the British Army to establish peace in Europe and the growth of the British Empire. In July 1828 Ebenezer Brown of Braendam passed away. His military career was founded as a surgeon, first in the 79th regiment and later the 30th regiment. He went with the army to the West Indies where malaria and yellow fever were to take a huge toll in life. He returned to take part in the British invasion of Egypt. He was busy behind the lines at the battle of Maida in Sicily and then served in the hugely successful peninsula campaigns that did much to destroy the myth of invincibility that had grown up around the Emperor Napoleon Bonaparte. Following the end of the Napoleonic wars after the battle of Waterloo in 1815 he returned to Thornhill bringing with him a Spaniard and a bear:

'which for its tricks on breaking loose one night had to be destroyed'.

I think he meant the bear.

Ebenezer enjoyed his retirement and tended his house (a listed building built in 1742 - 4 but 1790 in present form) and garden, but was always happy to revert to his role as doctor whenever the need arose.

Fig. 37 Braendam

A fine listed mansion now used as a school. This was the home of Ebenezer Brown, his Spanish friend and his wandering brown bear.

90

28. The Big Egg

The many impressive gardens of the district simply reflected the local interest and expertise in such matters. By the end of the nineteenth century the cattle markets had completely given way to horticultural interests. On 27 November 1891 30 people met following an advert and an address by Mr. R. Dawson, to form The Thornhill Horticultural Society. The group was dominated by local landowners but on the village committee was Robert Dawson, James McArthur and John Ferguson. They were to begin a society which still has a prominent role in the village today. The annual horticultural show took place in August and as usual was accompanied by a parade led by bands, a full dinner with speeches and a country dance ending off what was quickly to become one of the social events of the year. A high standard of horticulture very quickly became the norm. This can be seen by the success of Robert Dawson, who in September 1899 won some good prizes at the Glasgow Horticultural Show, then the leading show in the country.

It would be interesting to see if any of the present day affectionadoes can match some of the achievements of their ancestors. On 26 September 1890 John Johnston, a slater living in the Tanneree, had a hen who regularly laid an egg, mostly every day, with an average weight of 4 oz and measuring 9 inches round longitudinally and 6.5 ins in circumference. Mrs McQueen of Doig Street went one better in 1907. An egg laid by a hen belonging to her was sized 9 inches by 7.5 inches and had another complete egg inside it! Equally impressive was the 3 pound potato lifted by Mr. Dougal of Mid Borland in October 1913.

29. Disaster

It was not all plain sailing for the farming community, as the Thornhill weather was as unpredictable then as now. We hear of a lot of bad weather in 1858, including a whirlwind that swept through the village! Lightning can strike unpredictably and on 26 June 1913 it did. Four 2 year old heifers belonging to Mr Fisher of Easter Torr were killed by a single bolt when sheltering under a tree. This reminded people of the equally unpleasant weather in 1857 during which major disaster struck. On 5 September there was a terrible storm. James McQuarry was crossing a field just to the West of Thornhill with two friends when he was struck by lightning and died instantly, his body a charred black remnant. His two friends were also hit. Luckily one was just stunned but the other lay motionless and was given up for dead. Amazingly he recovered.

The area has also suffered periodic flooding. On 22 January 1909 much of the carse area was flooded and it is reported that many farms became isolated for several days and large numbers of livestock were drowned. Fortunately there were no human casualties. The village itself did not always escape such as on 26 August 1910 when there was waterlogging in the village with Burnhead and the Tannery houses being completely flooded.

30. "O would some pow'r the grace tae gi'e us, to see oursels as ithers see us"

The picture of the local area painted so far has been of a farming based society, not of grand wealth, but one in which community spirit had been nurtured and had grown and flowered. Other people agreed. A newspaper report of August 1885 written by 'Toledo' had this to say:

> *'Thornhill is unknown to many because of its difficult and poor access. If you have not been there I would say **go at once**. This is the pleasantest of pleasant villages, where you will be made welcome by a host of genuine country folk....... It has its famous Duig Street, 'east and west the toon', as the natives say.*
>
> *The entire population possess the trait by which a true Scot is known - hospitality.*
>
> *Another feature is its model schoolhouse judging from the smartness of the scholars. We are at once brought face to face with the fact that the training of the children is under a real dominie of the no-nonsense sort. His neat garden speaks volumes for his interest in flora. There are great gardeners in these parts - in fact agriculture, plain or ornamental is the ruling passion. It is no wonder that everything here produced is second to none.*
>
> *As a health resort Thornhill is foremost...and all the people require to make their village a busy one in winter and well frequented in summer is a railway'.*

Not all were entirely flattering about the village and perhaps we tended to be rather on the relaxed side at times. The editor of the Stirling Journal gently chided the village when in 1858 he wrote:

> *'Our friends in Thornhill must still be a leisurely sort of race - dwelling in Arcadian simplicity unaware of railways and electric telegraphs'*

News entries for the newspaper were not given at the speed which he desired. Perhaps the more relaxed approach led to some of the residents seeing their future elsewhere. There were plenty of options. With the spread of the British Empire Scots were destined to play a big part in manning and policing the new colonies. Consequently the spirit of emigration was ever present and Thornhill sent many of her sons and daughters to Canada, Australia, New Zealand and other parts. They were often encouraged. It was said in 1859:

'The spirit of emigration is very popular in this area. Few villages of a similar size have given more to the British colonies than Thornhill. They are all good hardy people. A few years ago most went to Canada but now most go to Australia and New Zealand'

Perhaps to redress this balance on 1 April 1910 Mr Hugh McKerracher, a travelling emigration agent from Canada, came to the area and stayed for two days. He used an impressive and gaudy decorated wagon with good horses to strengthen his message. He said:

"unparalleled opportunities await young men in agriculture and female domestic servants in Canada".

He obviously convinced some people and in 1911 a number of emigrants, such as the young Messrs. Yule and Thexton had presentations given to them as a farewell. A further five people left the village in 1912, all to Australia. The emigration trend was to continue, helped by public events and films well into the 1930's. Emigration may partly account for the population change in the parish. In 1862 the population of Kincardine was 2232 with 1284 in the Norrieston parish. By 1871 the Norrieston population had risen to 1484 with 348 families. However it was a very young population with 233 males and 240 females under 15. The children getting education at the time were 127 males and 121 females. Nevertheless by 1901 the population had fallen back to 1308 people.

MacFarlane

Fig. 38 Victorian Thornhill Group.

Daniel MacFarlane is seated second from the left on the front row of this impressive early photograph. Unfortunately none of the other people featured can be named.

95

31. Horsing about

It is remarkable how few major problems were evident at this time. The courts were not places towards which the village residents had a magnetic attraction. There were some domestic disputes but overall any problems that did occur stemmed from poverty or drink. In 1902 a resident of Hill Street, in dire financial straits, appeared before a Dunblane magistrate accused of keeping an unsanitary house. His house had defective drainage, earthen floors and was damp and filthy. The house was shut up and alternative accommodation sought for the residents.

The inadvisability of drink driving is well known to us all. The problem then was rather different. In 1907 John Anderson was fined ten shillings for being drunk in charge of a horse. The Sheriff said that:

'fortunately the horse was well capable of looking after himself'.

In 1914 William Ainslie had a collision on his buggy between Thornhill and Kippen. He was convicted of being drunk in charge of a horse and fined 20 shillings or 8 days prison. His defence was that he was short sighted and could not see where he was going!

Part 4. The Twentieth Century

32. Halcyon Days

The dawn of the twentieth century had no significant impact on the village. New Year celebrations were rather lively but for most it was business as usual. A few novelties began to appear. In June 1902 the children were delighted to hear the church bells ringing because it signified the end of the Boer War and this meant a day off school. They were not to know that a far more terrible war was looming on the horizon. No-one else suspected either as the standard of living in the village gradually began to improve. Only the month before laundry carts had begun to come to the village regularly and social occasions gave a welcome break from the daily grind. A new type of entertainment made a big impact. In May 1902 the Northern Cinematograph Company gave entertainment in the hall to a large audience thrilled by the movie pictures and the piano accompaniment. Local musicians did not feel threatened by this advance and in March 1908 a leap year dance took place heralded by songs from D. Donaldson and P Yule amongst others. It is likely that Duncan Drummond, fresh from his success in national piping competitions gave a tune or two as well.

McLachlan

Fig. 39 Thornhill East End 1920

Note the water pump in the street and the old weighing shed by the Commercial Hotel. The man standing by the street may be Mr. Sorley, the Commercial Hotel proprietor.

Even King Edward 7th almost made an appearance. In fact he visited Dunblane. Many spectators from Thornhill made the journey to see him in coaches hired from Mr. Ferguson in the Crown and Mr. Sorley of the Commercial Hotel. The village was gaily decorated even though the king was not coming to Thornhill, but those that went to Dunblane had an excellent view. There were other visitors to the village. Mr. Ord Pinder brought his travelling circus to the South Common but unfortunately torrential rain fell all day and the event fell rather flat. As militarism swept over Europe the only signs of increasing tension could be deduced from the setting up in 1908 of a local territorial force. This was only a small advance from the volunteer E company raised as long ago as 1891 and tenaciously promoted by Sergeant Moir, despite being assured that the company would collapse within three years! The militarism at large certainly did not dampen local enthusiasm when the property of William Sands, including among other things 10 properties on the Main Street, were sold in Stirling in 1908. Local bidding was intense and the properties were sold for between £100 - £200!

The fateful year 1914 began well in the village. A super celebration on Hogmanay had as its attractions a conjurer and a ventriloquist and was followed by a dance with Robert Dawson as MC that lasted until 3 am, and the celebrations were to continue for many more hours. The social whirl continued for some time. On 15 January the Established Church Choir held a social and dance with over 80 people in attendance. On the 5 February the turn came for the United Free Church Choir to have their social and over 70 people attended. The ploughing society held their annual competition on the 12 February with the usual social and dance to follow. Whist, which was very much a craze at this time, always attracted good numbers and on 5 March there was a whist drive and dance in the Commercial Hotel with over 70 present. The usual Young Farmers Picnic and Ploughman's Ball were great successes, as was the Horticultural Show. The social whirl was to continue almost unabated throughout the spring and early summer.

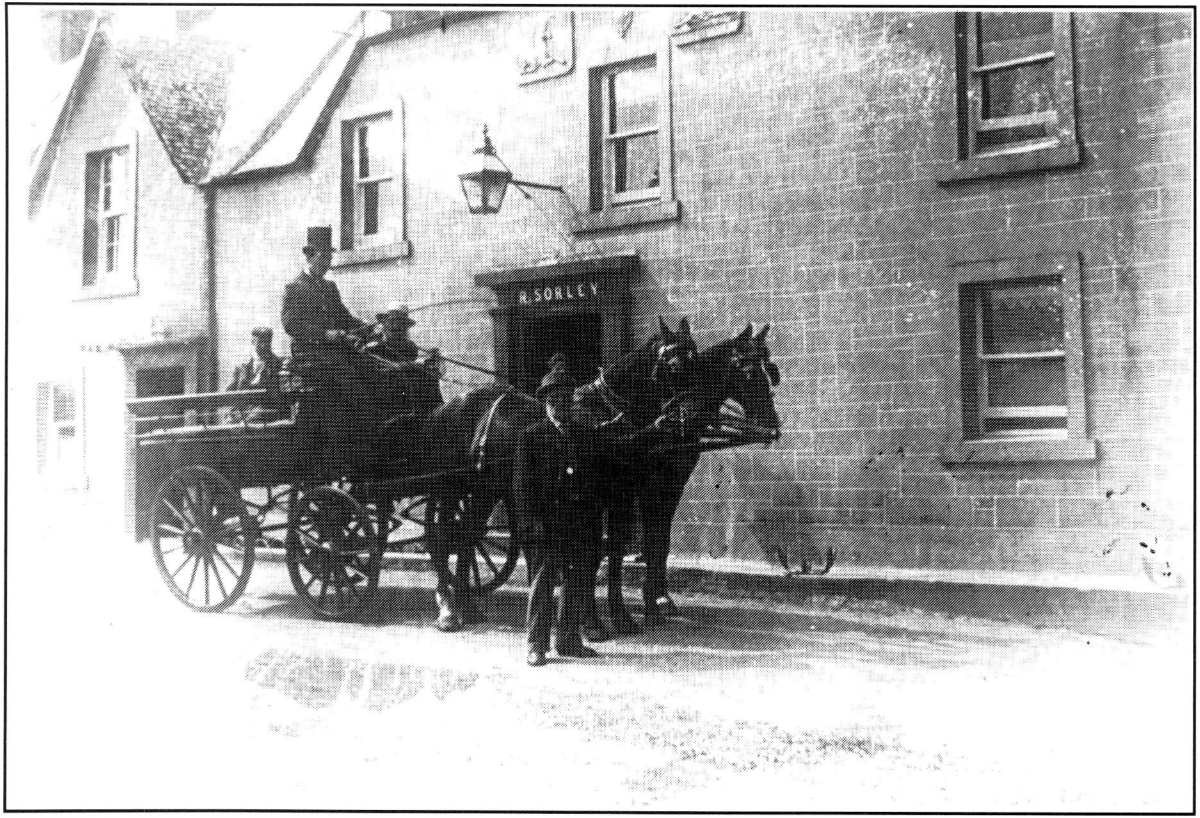

Sands / Diggens

Fig 40 The Commercial Hotel Taxi (early 20th century).

The well dressed coachman is Mr. William Dawson with Mr. Sorley looking on.

33. The Great War

One can imagine that John McLachlan would throw himself wholeheartedly into the social life of the village. He left Glasgow as a young boy and came to stay with his uncle in Hill Street. He went to school in the village and his uncle managed to get him a farming job at Goodiebank Farm. When the first world war broke out on 4 August 1914 there was great excitement throughout Scotland. Optimism was running rampant and it was confidently expected that the great adventure would be over by Christmas. The temptation was too much for the under - age John and he ran away to the recruiting office. He joined the 6th Battalion of the Black Watch but he was not destined return home by Christmas.

He was not destined to return home at all.

He spent a few months in Dundee on training in the depot. The battalion left Dundee on 22 April 1915 for further training in Bedford and then they moved onto the front lines in France. Incidents were all too common. In one a Stirling soldier left his trench to get water but in his absence a trench mortar scored a direct hit. When he returned he found the section commander and four of his men dead.

One was John McLachlan. He was seventeen years old.

Diggens

Fig. 41 John McLachlan

John is commemorated on the war memorial along with a further 20 of his friends and colleagues who lost their lives in those dreadful five years, a hard toll for a small village like Thornhill to bear.

Those who were unable to enlist began to find other ways of helping the war effort. Many locals were in reserved occupations, especially farming, but they flocked to the voluntary West Perthshire Recruit Battalion (Thornhill section) raised by J. Muir. Many others eagerly began to raise funds. A public meeting to raise funds for the 'Prince of Wales' Fund was well supported and within a month 50 pairs of socks, 4 mufflers and 7 shirts were sent off to France. There was no ploughing match this year, the first cancellation for over 50 years and many of the regular social events were to be suspended for the duration. However fund raising continued unabated with the children sending socks, etc. to the front and organising two school concerts for Belgium. In the village a territorial regiment camped in a field by the Commercial Hotel and regularly held marches down the Main Street. They requisitioned the horses from the Commercial Hotel and when the regiment left for the front the horses went with them. It was later said that almost all the men and horses were to become casualties.

There was a pleasant surprise on Christmas Day 1914 when the children whose fathers had gone on war service each received a present courtesy of the United States Government. That spurred them to renew fund raising efforts and in January 1915 alone over £54 was raised for the Prince of Wales Relief Fund.

The first local death in the war which brought home the grim reality of the situation was in May when Sergeant R. Milton Hamilton of Skeoch View was killed. Although he did not belong to the village his close relatives all did and he was well known by all.

Tragic news of Thornhill's sons and husbands was to be all too frequent over the next three years, following the horrors of such battles as the Somme and Passchendale, but those at home had to continue normal life as best they could. The local countryside and the paths that crossed them became more important to the village. The journey to work had always relied on cross country paths. It was considered to be quite normal for mill workers to walk over the moor to Deanston Adelphi Mill, do a long day's work, and then walk home afterwards. The children also enjoyed the paths free from the prying eyes of their parents. Nelly's Glen to the North of the village became a popular place and many picnics continued here during and after the war years.

However the normal social life was severely dented by the war and events normally had a fund raising aspect to them. In August 1918 a series of concerts for the armed forces was organised by the Reverend Mitchell but there was a severe shortage of home grown talent. The problem was solved by using artistes who were mainly the young ladies employed in gathering sphagnum moss from the undrained portions of the carse.

Financially things were very bad. Although Thornhill, being a country district, escaped the worst of food rationing, many people suffered from severe poverty. One must have an element of sympathy for a lady whose husband was at the front. She lived at Mucklehoney, 39 Main Street and was found guilty of ill-treating her five children by not giving them enough food and clothing and living in a verminous condition. She received 21 days in prison.

It was not all bad news. Thornhill had something to celebrate on 8 August 1918 when John Miller (Royal Scots) a son of the Millers of Spittalton Farm returned home. He had become a German prisoner of war, captured when his ammunition ran out in the big German advance of 1918. He escaped from near Cologne accompanied by a Russian soldier travelling by night and sleeping by day. He lived off the land, swam rivers and had numerous adventures. Finally a thunderstorm allowed them to slip through the German guards over the frontier into Holland from where he returned home to a heroes welcome.

THORNHILL WAR MEMORIAL.

Names of the Men who have Fallen.

William M. Cameron, John Cherrie, James Dick, Peter Duncanson, James Galbraith, R. Milton Hamilton, David Jenkins, William Moir, John S. Montgomery, James Morrison, Duncan M'Cowan, John M'Dougall, John M'Dougall, John MacLachlan, Donald M'Millan, David Renton, Robert M. Scott, Peter Sinclair, Charles S. Stewart, David M. Stewart, Michael Stewart.

Following the armistice of the 11 November 1918 the soldiers gradually began to return home to try to get back to a normal life. It must have been very difficult for some such as Gabriel Newton of Low Town. He was gassed in 1916 and wounded twice more during the war but still survived to tell the tale and became one of the most popular characters of the village in the post war years. Too many did not have the opportunity of returning.

Fig. 42 The War Memorial of 1919 with the names of those fallen in the Great War

Diggens

34. Tinkertown

Post Great War Thornhill tells a story of consolidation and gradual improvement in amenities and services, but it was to take time and did not appear without a fight.

Local services were not the top priority in people's minds immediately after the war. The first priority was to erect a memorial to honour the dead. On 15 May 1919 there was a public meeting to choose a suitable war memorial and on the 30 October 1920 the War Memorial was unveiled by the Earl of Moray with a guard of honour of local soldiers, commanded by Mr. Kilgour, the local schoolmaster. It was a touching ceremony for all the village and there were few dry eyes as the piper played the lament. Local returning soldiers were then treated to a formal welcome home party funded by a number of local events organised specifically for such an eventuality. Thornhill also managed to 'acquire' a German field gun and this was placed alongside the memorial. It was taken away in September 1936 and used for scrap metal because apparently the wheels were rotten.

It was not the only rotten thing in Thornhill according to the villagers. The problem of Thornhill's water supply was raised as early as 1899 but it was not until April 1921 that it was seriously discussed by Perthshire Council. The local complaint was that water was not in the houses but was all obtained by pumps. At least a gravity supply served most of the village but some people had to pump up the water a total of eight feet. The present system, set up by Lord Drummond in 1836 on the coming of age of his son, was now old and leaking badly, especially the Kennedy Well at the school and the Dastry Well in the North Common. It was to take 18 years of hard debate, innumerable public meetings, and tenacious lobbying by the council representatives before a new supply was finally installed to serve the houses of the village. It appeared in April 1939 using water from three reliable springs with new piping throughout, and all served by a large new storage tank on the Skeoch to the North of the village.

The returning soldiers had been promised a land fit for heroes but the reality proved rather different. There was just not enough money for the improvements needed in the village. During the recession of the 1920's and early 30's water supply was not the only problem. There was a considerable amount of poverty. The council recognised that the village was very poor. Average rates were comparatively low, indicating poor amenities, and 24 people were getting poor relief of one sort or another. There were five official resident poor; two were living on the common, two on the Main Street and one in a lodging house.

The village had also become a mecca for travelling people and others who had fallen on hard times. Hillview, commanding the top of the Kippen road and the cross-roads is a fine listed building (now converted into two separate houses) dating from the 18th Century. This was used as a boarding house for those in transit or of no permanent abode. There were also other houses in the village which were used as boarding houses or were subdivided into very small dwellings, giving what today we would consider to be grossly overcrowded conditions.

The two Commons were both causing problems as well. It was reported in 1926 and again in 1928 that gypsies from far and near were parking with caravans on the common. Twenty-one feuars complained of the dirty conditions resulting from this. In 1929 the squatter problem on the common was documented. There were 12 men, 10 women and 23 children living there with 32 in tents and 13 in vans. There were also five horses. It is important to remember that there were no conveniences of any sort available such as water, sewage disposal or power. Indeed a complaint to the council said that a plague of rats was in evidence and was getting into local houses. There was some action taken to sort out the squatter problem but complaints still surfaced from time to time. In October 1930 Mr. Duncanson, a council representative, noted that a horse belonging to a hawker was tethered on the common but it was later removed. Also in January 1931 it was reported that tinkers with a horse and 2 sons were living in the quarry. The council had by now become stricter in their regulations and they were moved on.

Waste disposal was another problem. There was no collection of household waste and it was disposed of as well as it could be. The Commons took the brunt of the waste. However in July 1934 the first 'scavenging' district group were set up to arrange for suitable waste disposal. It was agreed that there would be carting away of refuse twice weekly and any suitable rubbish would be spread and buried on the common or in the quarry. By now the quarry was almost totally filled in, mainly from waste ash from the houses. The Common itself was to be improved by the spreading of the existing dumps and the burial of tins, cutting of thistles and nettles, etc. There was also to be clearing and improvement of the ditches as the North Common still took a large part of the village sewage. The village would have to wait some time for a proper sewage treatment plant and for mains electricity.

Fig. 43 Hillview

This listed building has a strong claim to be the oldest existing house in the village, being situated at the top of the ridge and at the junction of routes. Near this house were the 'feeing' fairs of the last century and the cross (cross-roads) was the traditional place where important news was announced. The house itself has been used for many functions, not all legal, although it is as a boarding house early this century that it is best known.

Fig. 44 The war memorial in the 1920's

The rural scene is very different from today as the view is restricted by building and trees. The German Field Gun was to remain on this site until 1936.

Diggens

35. Heavenly Thanks for locals and visitors

The picture painted of the inter war years tends to give the impression of a village where poverty and squalor were never far away. This may be the official picture but local residents have a very different memory. The fact that the railway never came to Thornhill meant that its growth was modest and by 1935 the population was only 650. Its relative inaccessibility meant that community spirit had been allowed to grow and nurture for two hundred years and was strong indeed. It was considered quite normal to help each other, and people went to extraordinary lengths to give support when it was needed. They knew that in turn they would receive equal help and support and often all that was necessary was a 'thank you'. The very high level of social activity has already emerged as a feature of Victorian Thornhill, but this did not die with the passing of the century. Dances, socials and community meetings of all types remained an integral and important part of village life until recent years, and even today a high level of social involvement remains. Of course there were disputes, but the abiding memory of residents   tends overwhelmingly to be of good times, a happy and friendly people and a village at peace with itself.

McLachlan

Fig. 45 The Crown Hotel

This photograph taken in 1956 shows a neat line in brickwork at the front of the hotel. The cottage to the left has now become part of the hotel. Note the signs on the front and roof, and also the television aerial, one of the first in the village.

36. Tourism

This is the Age of the motor car and today a large number of Thornhill residents travel to work outwith the village. However it is difficult if you have to rely on public transport. It has never been easy, although bus routes used to serve the village much more frequently than now. There was also the train. The nearest stations were Kippen and Doune. At least there was a regular service to Doune Station. The Lion and Unicorn Hotel (The Commercial Hotel until 1951) had a number of stables. The Ferguson family (who owned both hostelries in Thornhill in the early part of this century) instigated a horse bus service which ran to Doune Station twice a day. This was no doubt useful to local inhabitants, but it served another purpose as it brought tourists to the village. Most visitors were Glaswegians escaping from the city for short breaks and the Commercial and Crown Hotels were frequently full to capacity, especially during the Glasgow Fair. Perhaps it was the difficulty of getting accommodation or perhaps it was the welcoming nature of the village but a significant number of houses on the Main Street were now owned by Glasgow people and were often used as holiday retreats.

The peace and quiet of the village and its attractive surrounding scenery would have been the main attractions for the tourists but there were some other enticements. The house at 55 Main Street was the Bank of Scotland, but was also used as a small private museum with mainly ceramics on display.

Fig. 46 55 Main Street
The former Bank of Scotland and also a small ceramic museum

Fig. 47 28 Main Street

This was the former British Linen Bank

The present Crown Hotel Bar was once a separate cottage and contained an antique shop. This was supplemented by a further antique shop at number 37/39 Main Street. Prior to the antique business here this 18th century listed building housed a number of colourful characters. The house itself was once five separate dwellings, let out to tenants. People remember a boot and shoe repairer called Tom Dow and for a long time the lane across the street leading to the South Common was known as 'Tam Dow's Loan'. He kept up a small garden there and woe betide anyone who picked his flowers. Also living in the block was Kenny the Painter, who is remembered as a fine craftsman who specialised in gilding. Kenny thought nothing of walking six miles to work and another six back again in the evening, and he still had time to show off his prowess at ice skating by cutting his name with his skates on the ice rink with impressive accuracy. Also fondly remembered was 'Bassie' who sold ice cream as he travelled round the village on his donkey.

Fig 48 37 / 39 Main Street

One of the candidates for the oldest house in the village, but most likely dating from the 1780's. This house, now extensively altered, is a listed building which once housed almost 20 people in five separate let dwellings.

Other diversions for the tourist and local alike would be the Bowling Green by the Commercial Hotel, opened by the Fergusons about 1912. Nearby, where now stands Norrieston Place, was a putting green. In the cold winters the Curling Pond was in full use on the 'Lug' in the North Common. Indeed the Curling Hut still stands as a small brick building at the bottom of a garden to the West End of the North Common. The Commons themselves were of great value to local and visitor alike despite the squatter problems. Many residents still exercised their ancient rights and used the land for grazing and herding cattle, especially the North Common. A converted barn which once housed six cattle can still be seen at the west end of the North Common.

There was grazing on the South Common too but recreation was becoming more important. The Common was badly drained and the open ditches were not ideal for developing the silky skills we now associate with the football team. The dependency culture played no part in 1930's Thornhill and locals, all volunteers, got together and formed the King George V Jubilee Committee. They had the task of levelling and draining the Common, and forming the children's play park. By June 1936 John Miller on behalf of the football club got permission to tile and drain the Common for a permanent pitch. The football team play there to this day.

The South Common is now split by warehousing but on this site was once an orchard. Winters were cold but at least some of the summers were hot and there was a roaring local trade in strawberries. Thornhill was (and still is) noted for soft fruit production and the area to the West and North of Hill Street was all strawberry fields. This provided a useful source of employment for the youngsters of the village. The fields were busy by 6 am in early summer with children picking the fruit prior to going to school. William Ure at Cambo Cottage, Low Town, was the gathering centre for strawberries and soft fruit, but here the owner had a new innovation........greenhouses.

Early fruit you may think, and indeed there was, but during the war he found another rather novel use for his glasshouses.......... Thornhill became a boat building centre, and a number of lifeboats were constructed.

Where were the boats launched?

McLachlan

Fig. 49 The Bogs, Thornhill

The football pitch prior to its movement to the present site. The local boys are seen enjoying a game, although those in bare feet may regret shooting the heavy leather ball. In the background left can be seen 2 Low Town, one of the oldest houses in the village. The scene up to the Main Street is almost unchanged although it cannot be easily seen today because of the houses now built on Bells Brae (Kippen Road).

37. Shops and Services

When the Easter School building ceased to be a school in 1872 it became the village hall. This old hall, called the Montgomery Hall, was used for anything and everything. Meetings, concerts and the weekly hugely popular moving pictures packed the hall. It served its purpose well - at least until the time came for the village dances. They were always popular and the building rocked with the energetic strains of strathspeys and reels. Unfortunately the building was not the only thing that rocked. There were many heads that rocked as well because of a pole in the middle of the dance floor. The local technique was to avoid the pole during particular wild flurries of such dances as 'strip the willow' and the 'eightsome reel'. The technique, gathered by years of experience, tended to fail as the evening wore on!

By 1937 the old building was beginning to feel its age and there was a public meeting on whether to purchase it for the village and continue with it as the village hall. The decision was positive and fund raising began immediately for renovation. The war came a little too early and there was still work to do but the hall seemed to stand the pounding until it was used to billet the visiting troops. The troops lived, ate and slept in the hall and to do this they built ablutions at the south end of the building. It was clear by the end of the war that something was amiss, and it was suspected that the building of ablutions had at the south end had undermined the whole wall. The problem became clearer in 1947 when the wall fell down! This was the end of the Montgomery Hall and the whole building was demolished and is now a car park.

Shopping and services were much more in evidence too. There were two banks. The Bank of Scotland has already been mentioned (see fig. 46), but this was in competition with another bank, the British Linen Bank, at Osborne House opposite the Crown Hotel (fig. 47). Other shops at various times during this century have included the Sands General Store at Slatehaa (fig. 17), and back into the last century this was also the Post Office. The Post Office later moved position to the corner house on the cross-roads (now demolished during road widening) opposite the general store, before moving to 54 Main Street. The present building was purpose built for the task and had taken over by 1939. 69 / 71 Main Street was also a General Store and Bookmaker, with a Grocer at 41 Main Street, a further Grocer at 34 Main Street and McLarens the Butcher at 44 Main Street.

The present butcher, Alexander Gray, occupied 47 Main Street before moving to its present site, which in turn was probably a Chemist at the end of the last century. The Abattoir business was rather haphazard and the killing of animals was done in the village. There were three killing houses to be found. One was at the bottom of the garden of Grays the Butcher, by the North Common, and on the opposite side a further one was at the bottom of the Loan by the South Common. The Commercial Hotel had their own behind their premises.

Fig. 50 showing the position of the killing house

The 'killing house' stood on the ground to the left of the road. The road itself forms one of the entrances to the North Common from the Main Street, and may be one of the original 'cross wynds' of 1696.

It was even possible to buy all your clothes in the village at McNab's the Tailors situated where the Dykes Lawnmower shop now is. Fond memories are given of Johnson's Newspaper Shop situated where the garden area stands today in front of the Post Office. The Johnson's shop was a wooden construction built in the style of the settlers' houses of the American 'wild west' hick towns. It was said to be very popular, perhaps because of the enormous cast iron stove used to heat the shop in winter. It enabled customers to gently toast, even in the middle of winter as they passed their time in the shop. This newsagent later moved up the street to take the more permanent premises of 34 Main Street and the famous building was no longer needed.

The Scoulars began business with a small cycle shop and built this up to open a garage on the site of where the present day Dykes Chain Saw and Lawnmower Workshop stands. The Scoulars caused a few early gasps with their antics on their bicycles. It is well remembered seeing Jack Scoular hurtling down Bells (The Kippen Road) Brae. This is not unusual you may think, but he did it on his penny farthing bicycle, which, of course, had no brakes.

113

He used his bicycles to good effect in other ways when he set up a mobile smithy, which was basically a bicycle with bellows and other accoutrements. Jack was a well-known practical joker and enjoyed his outing to vote at Doune with Mr. Allan, a well-known local artist. They travelled to Doune in style on a motor cycle and sidecar and there saw the Duchess of Atholl, who was canvassing as the local Conservative candidate. She was obviously busy because the two of them slapped a red parking ticket on her limousine and no doubt sat back with glee to watch her reaction. Her words go unrecorded!

As the mechanised variety of transport took over Scoulars Garage were the proud possessors of the first petrol pump in the area. However by 1 April 1932 the local Perth Council were less impressed. They complained that the petrol pump on the pavement of Main Street was causing an obstruction and was likely to cause injury to pedestrians as they were forced to step out onto the road. Other services in the village included the carpenter, cartwright and undertakers owned by Donald McBeth at 19 Main Street. In later years there also was the Joiners shop at 66 Main Street, originally owned by William Sands. William Forrester then joined with him and the shop ultimately ended up as James Forrester and Alex. Montgomery. Local tradition asserts that a whisky still, one of many, was situated on this site during Thornhill's 'whisky period'. The still is long gone, but the house's role continued to interest the villagers, as it was used for storage of munitions in World War Two. There was great excitement shortly after the war ended when the bomb disposal, police, etc. suddenly descended on the village. They had come to diffuse a large quantity of arms found abandoned near the house and the excitement was fortunately short lived.

38. Carts and Parrots

In addition to the shops the everyday needs of the village were served by mobile services. On The Hill was based William McLay, the Coal Merchant. Coal was brought in by railway to Kippen and it was collected by horse and cart. William then went round the village on his huge Clydesdale horse and cart delivering to customers. He was in competition with Davie Stewart living at 67 Main Street who ran his coal business in addition to running a tannery. Fresh milk was also available from the Jamiesons of Norrieston, delivered to your door. Their customised cart had a huge tank which was filled with fresh milk. The customers would bring their jugs and containers and fill up from a tap at the back of the tank.

Diggens

Fig. 51 Mr. John Miller and his fish cart

Mrs Agnes McLachlan who owned the Lodging House on Hill Street (and lived in a small private part) came round the village with her 'bowl cart' containing china and bric-a-brac. Mr. John Millar, who was also from the Hill ran a fresh fish cart service (see fig. 51).

Tom Newton was well known for his tendency to walk round the village and the local area singing and playing his violin. In 1930 At the age of 83 years he was walking back from Kippen when he fell dead from a seizure, and the village mourned the loss of a character liked by all. However he was only the last in a long line of similar characters who enlivened our streets and our lives.

One of the best known was 'Kippen Jock'. John Robertson, better known as 'Kippen Jock,' had a roaming disposition and went round the village (usually accompanied by a crowd of boisterous youths) with a home - made trolley, made by rigging together two bicycle wheels which ran on a well worn axle attached to a pair of wheels of different dimensions. The wheels were never straight on his cart because they were:

"A' the better to cope with the road"

McLachlan

Fig. 52 Kippen Jock

Jock is posing on the South Common along with his famous cart, although the wheels here seem similar in size. The trees in the background mark the borders of an orchard. Within the boundaries of this orchard stood the last thatched cottage in Thornhill. The building immediately behind Kippen Jock is now demolished, although the cottage to the right remains.

116

Jock, his end hastened by a kick from his horse, died at his home in Hill Street and is buried in Norrieston Churchyard (see Appendix 4). Kippen Jock was not far wide of the truth regarding the roads, because they were often in a terrible state. The plight of the Hill has already been mentioned but even the Main Street was not taken over and surfaced until October 1891. The Hill had to wait until 14 December 1937 and this was only after a long campaign by the parish councillors. Astonishingly when the road was finally taken over it was with an apology from Perth Council, because they had agreed to maintain the road in 1891 along with Main Street but amazingly they had mislaid the minute, or some other internal problem arose.

It took 46 years to rectify the mistake!

Until the surfaces were made up earlier this century everybody was responsible for their own pavement. Consequently some were flagged, some cobbled, some had chippings and some had nothing.

Kippen Jock was probably right! Walking around the village on the long winter's nights must have been hazardous. There was little to worry about in terms of traffic but the pavements were excellent for breaking ankles. This was made worse by the fact that there was only one gas light outside the Crown Hotel to light all the Main Street. This light is still there but is now converted to electricity.

The social events were perhaps not on the scale of the huge gymnastic games of the last century but were popular and well attended nevertheless. Jack Johnston was the town crier and helped to promote attendance enormously as he paraded the village making sure that no-one missed the news of the day. The clubs and societies were similar to those of today but still formed an impressive list. Active were the Band of Hope under the indefatigable Mrs Connel, the Nursing Association, a very active WRI, the Church Guild, Football Club (a thriving and successful female football team was also active), the Curling and Bowling Clubs, the Gun Club, Music Clubs, the Scouts and Guides and many more. The hugely popular whist drives were often held in the Commercial Hotel and were enlivened by a parrot which mimicked everything. History has a strange way of repeating itself, as in 1994 the present proprietor arrived home - with a parrot. There was more visiting entertainment too such as the dramas put on by the West Highland Players in 1932. In April 1935 even Ord Pinder (remember him)? arrived back on the South Common with his visiting circus. He seemed fated on his Thornhill visits. The circus seemed to go all right but it was later reported that Jeannie Harris whose house backed onto the Common had Pinder's horses breaking into her garden and doing considerable damage. Mr. Pinder had to pay damages but Jeannie was probably rather relieved that it was only the horses from the circus that made the breakout!

At this time a Mr. Featherstone from Glasgow had made a big impact in the village. By January 1934 he had acquired 18 properties in the village and was to get more before he

117

moved to Callander. Not all in the village supported his actions and he was certainly a stern landlord. However others have thanked him for rescuing some older properties that may well have fallen into a state of severe disrepair had he not rehabilitated them. Some of the young people found him a rather more terrifying proposition.

The Manse (Blair Hill), a listed building of 1848, was bought by him and was re-christened by the youngsters 'Featherstone Hall'.

The large beech hedge around the garden caused no problem, and neither did the churchyard almost next door. However problems did arise when Mr. Featherstone decided to put statues in his garden. During the long winter nights the children would quicken their pace slightly as they walked past the churchyard. They relaxed on passing as they felt more safe, only to be severely jolted as suddenly they saw black figures, where previously there were none, rearing over the hedge of Featherstone Hall. The statues are no longer present and the Norrieston Corner has returned to its more peaceful state.

McLachlan

Fig. 53 The Hill or Hill Street:

This street, once a cul de sac, has a number of fine 18th century houses, but the road was not made up until 1937. This photograph is from an earlier period and the state of the road and pavement leaves much to be desired.

Fig. 54 The Manse

The former manse, now called Blair Hill, is a listed building dating from 1848. It was nicknamed Featherstone Hall when Mr. Featherstone owned a lot of property in the village in the 1930's.

39. Industry and invention

Employment was still dominated by farming but there were some alternatives. There was the smithy at the west end of the village where the present Dykes Garage now stands. This superseded the small smithy to the West end of the Main Street which was known as Balmoral Cottage. Next door was 'The Palace'. Tradition has it that Queen Victoria on one of her numerous trips to the Trossachs stopped at this point to get a horse's shoe replaced - hence the significance of the names.

To the East was a further smithy at Corshill Cottage just outside the village. This was the home of the MacFarlanes, so noted for longevity. They were also noted for their skills and several generations of master blacksmiths trained and worked here. Daniel MacFarlane, the famous centenarian, was also something of an inventor and became recognised world wide in his field when he invented a system to eliminate dust from alternators. His invention must have cleared the air and the minds hereabouts because a few years later, in December 1934, Alexander Moir of Little Ward was delighted to receive a £50 prize from the Highland Agricultural Society for inventing a roller attachment for mowers.

The Mill at Cessintully was to remain an important part of local employment until its closure in 1956. Without a doubt the Mill at Cessintully is one of the oldest sites in the area but the old building was mainly demolished in 1853.

McLachlan

Fig. 55 The Cessintully Mill Wheel.

The huge metal mill wheel is now no longer on this site and the Cessintully Mill, perhaps the oldest continuously settled site in the area, is now a private house.

121

The Smithy Thornhill.

80787

Fig. 56 The Smithy, Thornhill

McLachlan

An enhanced photograph dating from the early years of this century showing the Smithy at the Western end of the village. This building is now demolished. Note the old plough by the outhouse. The Aberfoyle road is in the foreground.

MacFarlane

Fig 57 The Crosshill Smithy 'Gang'

Daniel MacFarlane is to the right of the picture and Sandy MacFarlane, the last smith to work here, is in the centre of the picture. The smithy in the background is now converted to provide excellent holiday accommodation.

The new mill was a three storey building with a high technology waterwheel. The water wheel was an overshoot which means that water hit the top of the wheel and therefore power was transferred from above. This was said to be more powerful. The lade stored water and gave it height and a sluice from the lade took the water over the wheel and back into the Cessintully Burn.

The mill concentrated on rolled oats but was prepared to mill anything required by local farmers. Work was often hard and the damp hot conditions made it a health hazard at times. It was hard on the boots too as the continually wet floors tended to rot them all too quickly. When the hammer mills became easily obtainable after the war it was the beginning of the end for the mill, and today it is used mainly as a garage and for storage.

The magnificent water wheel has now gone as has the round mill ring for the horses. Even the lade has sprung a leak and is often dry in the summer. Nevertheless it is easy to imagine, amid the pleasant and tranquil surroundings where otters from the Goodie Burn frequently visited, what a scene of activity has existed here for over 600 years. It has had its share of drama but fortunately not of the tragic kind. John Millar, one of the last millers here remembers well when all the produce to be milled was brought in by horse and cart. Sometimes things did not always go to plan, especially where strong willed horses were concerned. A particular Clydesdale was a model worker when his master was watching. On this day the master was distracted and the horse took its chance, decided that was enough for the day and started to make its way home. The owner chased the massive Clydesdale along as far as the Kirk, where fortunately he caught the beast, probably just in time before his language earned him a severe reprimand from the minister.

A few years later on a bitterly cold morning during the second world war John lit a fire, as he usually did, using straw and corn husks in a desperate attempt to get warm. As his circulation gradually came back he was amused to see the Army arriving in haste thinking the place was on fire. They retreated rather embarrassed about somewhat of an overreaction, but perhaps they had been told about the fire at Norrieston Farm in July 1934. The fire which originated in a bothy quickly spread and destroyed a wing of the house containing the bothy, a scullery and a milk house.

1934 and early 1935 were not good years to remember for some local farmers as they were to see three dreadful accidents. In April 1934 Angus Ferguson, the farmer of Braendam, became caught in the mechanism of an engine and suffered a double fracture of both legs. By February 1935 two remarkably similar accidents at nearby farms were both to end in loss of life for the poor unfortunates, almost giving truth to the Norrieston legend of death happening in threes. Indeed life was still hard and officialdom very strict as a local boy found out in 1933 when he succumbed to temptation and stole a watch from the Corshill Smithy. His punishment was a hefty fine, far beyond what he could pay, or 20 days' imprisonment.

40. Keep the home fires burning

The years leading up to 1938 gave no clue to the impending crisis. The Amateur Dramatic Society led by Sandy Scoular managed to perform such light hearted sketches as 'the lunatic and others' and 'paddy and the ghost'. The new Thornhill Jazz Band (of Alex. Miller, Jimmy Douglas and Mhairi Miller) continued to entertain and the village craze for fancy dress showed no sign of abating. For example on 24 July 1938 a fancy dress parade in aid of the hall extension fund was held on the South Common and was followed by a dance in the hall. Winners of the main prizes were; lady's prize to Miss B Williamson (lady in waiting), the lady in a male costume to Nurse MacFarlane, the best comic costume to Messrs. McLachlan, Donaldson and Petrie (The Three Macs) and the children's winner was Miss O McGregor.

Spence

Fig. 58 A village at play: the fancy dress competition.

Thornhill society was adept at making its own entertainment, and the fancy dress party was common and always popular. This photograph from the late 1920's gives a flavour of such events.
Left to Right: E. Spence, L. Stewart, J. MacFarlane, P. Ainslie, D. Stewart, N. MacFarlane.

125

Diggens / Spence

Fig. 59 The Cowboys arrive in Town. Jock Miller in the fancy dress.

The usual clubs and societies had continued and many, such as the Women's Rural Institute, were positively thriving. An article in the Stirling Journal on the appalling persecution of Jews in Germany was noted but did not dampen the optimistic attitude. Patriotism was rife and when the massive new Trans-Atlantic liner, the Queen Mary, had her maiden voyage down the Clyde, three buses full of villagers from Thornhill were there to cheer her on. Even an outbreak of typhoid did not cause undue alarm, being blamed on watercress, but the mood began to change in late 1938 and 1939 as the prospect of war began to loom. The football club were the first to show the mood change as they staged their own rehearsal of war with Germany in a match against Balfron on 25 July 1938 on the South Common. A keenly fought contest ultimately boiled over and a series of free fights took place leading to the home spectators invading the pitch. The pitch was finally cleared and the referee wanted to continue but Balfron refused and so the game was abandoned. In a year's time the whole league was to be postponed as the young people of the area had an altogether more serious battle to fight. By March 1939 plans had been put in place and the village was busy rehearsing black out procedures which were to last almost six years. April saw the distribution of gas masks to all the villagers.

In September war was declared. The Stirling area almost immediately got a number of evacuees from Glasgow and by 7 September 90 evacuees had arrived in the village by bus. They were given tea in the school and then they moved on to their temporary homes in local houses and farms. The blackout was in full force, and the school was on a double shift with the hours being 9 - 12 for locals and 1 - 4 PM for evacuees. A second supply of evacuees arrived from Glasgow on Thursday 12 October. They came to Doune Station and were conveyed by bus to the school.

Although there were now a large number of evacuated children in the village very many of them were to stay only a short time. Their parents, mainly from Glasgow, visited them and often decided to take the risks and bring them back home. The few Clydebank parents were to regret that decision, as the blitz was destined to strike their town in just the very next year.

It was realised that despite the planning no-one actually knew what the procedure was in the event of an Air Raid warning and so the following instructions were transmitted in local newspapers and advertising posters in the village:

'The warning will be transmitted by the ringing of church bells reinforced by special constables blowing sharp blasts on their whistles. If poison gas is suspected a hand rattle will be used. All people to remain inside until the all clear is sounded'.

Fortunately these precautions were never necessary for real. However there were mistakes, especially when the Home Guard, based in the Masonic Lodge, had an exercise involving a simulated invasion and the bells were rung. Unfortunately no-one told the rest of the village it was an exercise!

The confusion that reigned then was as nothing however compared to the small earthquake that shook the village in February 1940 when most were convinced the bombing had started. It had not, but Miss Peggy Douglas of Callander Road had joined the ambulance unit based in the Port of London and she was not so lucky. During the bombing of 1941 she was commended for great personal bravery. She dealt with casualties at three separate incidents and:

'showed courageous devotion to duty in the face of great personal danger'

In 1941 the village was designated as an official rest centre in the event of severe bombing in Scotland and very quickly the village had begun to take on the appearance of an armed camp. The Cheshire Regiment was billeted in the village with the Commercial Hotel used for officers and the Crown Hotel used for NCO's. The WRI was kept busy staffing the soldiers' canteen and organising entertainment for the troops. Behind the Crown is the old coach house which could well be one of the original buildings of Thornhill. It is now listed and used as a store but then acted as the NCO's mess.

Fig. 60 The Crown Coach House

The old coach house behind the Crown Hotel is now a listed building and may well be one of the original buildings of the village. Today it is used as a store but it has had a number of other functions in the past such as an NCO's mess.

The officer's cook was well remembered, but not for his cooking. His red face shone like a beacon and he was none too concerned about hygiene. However the Cheshires' seemed to thrive on it and became well integrated with the village, especially when they organised their picture shows. These affairs were ticket only but it was usually possible to get a ticket off a soldier. One village youngster whose favourite pastime was to tease the soldiers as a result failed to get a ticket one evening. His revenge was to disconnect the generator supply to the temporary cinema!

chaos ensued.

Needless to say there were no pictures that night and the young lad in question kept his head down for a few weeks!

The Royal Army Ordnance Corps also had a large presence in the village and both the Hill and the Low Town were used as wagon parks. There were a number of ammunition compounds in the surrounding area, including by the North Common, along the Doune Road and also at Blairhoyle, where remnants can still be seen built into a wall. Locals watched with amusement as the Home Guard, ordered to defend the ammunition dump on the North Common, decided to dig a slit trench for cover. The North Common is notorious for its poor drainage and indeed has a number of rare plants as a result. It is not ideal trench country however!

The Guard found out the hard way and groaned with frustration as the trench slowly filled with water.

The war made a huge impact on all groups in the village. Thornhill was not slow to provide a steady stream of recruits for the war but there were not so many agricultural workers as before and fewer could be spared. The 'dig for victory' campaign was well received, as one would expect in an area with such strong agricultural and horticultural traditions and in 1942 a visit to the village was organised by the WRI from the Ministry of Food. A series of cookery demonstrations were given and a talk entitled 'How to make best use of garden produce' was well received, although most in the village were no slouches at this ancient skill.

Many of the old soldiers were active in the Home Guard, and the picture presented was very different from the 'Dads Army' cliché.

It was noted that the Home Guard:

> *'presented an inspiring sight, with all looking very fit and smart'*

Even the schoolchildren formed their own army complete with pretend officers and NCO's. The ladies of the village excelled themselves in fund raising and comfort support for the armed services and very impressive sums of money were raised on a regular basis.

Fig. 61 The Home Guard

McLachlan

The Home Guard complete with Pipe Band march down the Main Street of Thornhill. Notice the delight of the children on the right of the picture as they carefully copy the drummers. The two posts to the mid left of the picture were road sign posts. All the road signs had been removed in order to confuse any German Parachutists who might appear in the area!

A constant stream of produce left the village throughout the war. For example in April 1941 alone the ladies of the village presented to the Red Cross:

43 pairs of socks
24 body belts
2 pairs of gloves
1 pair of mittens
12 sets of pyjamas
5 vests
4 shirts.

Fund raising was equally impressive. An example was 'Warship Week' in May 1942. This was opened by A K Muir of Blair Drummond. Although over £5000 had already been raised by the village the week before a special effort was still made. There was a procession led by a Pipe Band followed by the Home Guard and Civil Defence Service, the Special Police, WVS and Girls' Guildry. After the procession a football match between the local Home Guard and the Royal Army Service Corps took place at Blairhoyle followed by a dance. Other functions during the week included the inevitable fancy dress parade (winners were Mrs McPhail [highlander] and William Dawson [Victorian lady], and for the children Elma Dick [Dutch girl]), a jumble sale and 2 further concerts and dances. By the end of the week Thornhill had raised over £12,200; a magnificent total. The 'Wings for Victory' week in 1943 raised £17,282 - far in excess of the target and the 'salute the soldier' week in June 1944 was equally successful. The target was set at £10000 but the amount actually raised was £16250.

The long years of the war dragged on and anxious families waited for news of their sons from the various fronts. Tragic news was too frequent as two Thornhill residents lost their lives during the war and a number of others were injured. Occasionally more cheering news came through such as when Donald Beaton was promoted to Sergeant in the RAF and mentioned in dispatches for his bravery in action, and Walter Stewart of Slatehaa, serving with the Commandos, was awarded the oak leaf decoration. Many of the wounded were tended in Blair Drummond Auxiliary Hospital and the Girls Guildry expended a great deal of time in organising diversions for them such as beetle drives, quizzes, etc.

The village had done its bit and more for the war effort and richly deserved the celebrations that occurred in May 1945 on the occasion of VE Day. The village was decorated with flags and bunting throughout, and two effigies of Hitler, one in Hill Street and one on a bonfire in the Common were burned with glee. A special service in the church was held followed by a very well attended dance in the church hall. The band comprised all local players and three pipers were also present. Just before midnight the whole party, led by the pipers, went to the South Common. The bonfire was lit at one minute past midnight by Private. N McDiarmid, a serviceman on leave. A quiet prayer was said for all the people who had lost their lives in the war, and then all trooped back to the hall for the dancing and celebrations which were to last throughout the night.

41. Post War Thornhill

The modern history of the village is a task for a future chronicler, and is outside the scope of this book. Nevertheless a brief resume of developments may be of interest to the reader

Four local people had lost their lives during this war and for the second time this century the village had to pick itself up and get back to normal life. The immediate history of the village, post 1945, was mainly concerned with this aim.

Village services still dominated the post war agenda. Fortunately there had been some movement. The new water supply was now in operation and the campaign for bringing electricity to the village, which began before the war, had brought success when street lights were first installed in 1947. However it was to take some time before both water and electricity were installed in all the houses. The Commons were still causing some problems. The council had taken over the South Common with the agreement of the feuars but a similar scheme was rejected for the North Common, despite comments that it was an eyesore with a minor gypsy problem and a more serious problem of straying livestock. It was not surprising that it was called an eyesore because at that time the village sewage was directed into its ditches and drains. The animals hardly helped matters. Council minutes for 11 July 1946 complain that cattle had broken into gardens and cattle and horses were straying onto the road from the North Common. The council agreed to take action on this and also clear the ditches whose banks had been broken by livestock. Much of the western portion of the Common was cleared and later levelled but had no further development. The Common now has a very different role in the village. It is rare to find unimproved land near any urban settlements in Scotland and in the North Common Thornhill has an almost unique asset. It is now home to about 150 native plant species and is frequented from time to time by rare birds and animals. Its chief role is acting as a 'lung' for the residents. Whether it is for the children to have open rough land to explore or whether it is for exercising the dog or the horse it is an important open space.

By 1946 the village began its campaign to have a new drainage and sewerage system and the present arrangements came into effect in 1951. It was sorely needed to cope with both existing housing and the new housing beginning to appear.

The Main Street had stubbornly stuck to its old ways with most houses known by the name of their occupants, either present or past. Locals had no problem with this and the custom is still very much with us today despite all the houses being given numbers in 1950.

Civic pride has already featured in this chronicle and was still evident in more recent times. A Canadian visitor to the village in 1967 had toured the whole area and wrote that:

'Thornhill was the tidiest place we saw, with not so much as a bus ticket to mar the Main Street'.

This was encouraging and very much needed in view of the relative poverty still evident in the neighbourhood. By 1979 it was reported that Thornhill had too many sub standard houses with 16 either under a demolition order or proposed demolition. The Thornhill Development Plan then came into being to improve the current housing stock and build new houses in gap sites in Low Town and Doig Street. The plan also involved landscaping, an improvement to the sewerage system and the development of a village clinic. These developments almost bring us up to date and reflect the very considerable improvement in the outward appearance of Thornhill. The few new houses in the village are in great demand and it would still be very surprising to find so much as a bus ticket littering the street, although it must be said that the frequency of buses does tend to make this even more unlikely!

The summer sees the village at its best. Miss Graham, once of Corsehill, began the window box scheme. Today the Main Street is often ablaze with colour in the summer as the majority of the houses still continue and develop this tradition despite perhaps a majority of residents now travelling some distance to work outwith the immediate area. Nevertheless the village is far from a dead commuter town. Indeed a resident of 100 years ago would recognise a lot of aspects. The production of soft fruit continues to thrive in the area and agriculture remains a central part of the local economy with some specialisations such as an international reputation for horse breeding. Any visitor to the giant onion or leek competitions would gasp at the size and quality of the vegetables, and will be left in no doubt that horticulture remains popular and strong.

The tourist industry remains prominent with many visitors now staying in the village area at local bed and breakfast establishments and the caravan park. The Trossachs Trail, which passes through the village, is likely to increase the popularity of the local area still further.

The multiplicity of local clubs and activities remain strong. The age mix and social harmony together with an active and friendly village environment means that the comments of 'Toledo' made 100 years ago are still not far short of the mark when he described the village as:

'the pleasantest of pleasant villages'

Appendix 1: Norrieston Churchyard

Earlier this century the Reverend George Williams made some observations on some of the older stones in Norrieston Churchyard following on from research by James McGregor in the mid 19th century. The Scottish Genealogical Society continued the study in 1974 but noted that many of the inscriptions were unreadable and some of the stones had been removed, when the council took over the churchyard, to enable mowing machines to be used. It is therefore worth recording the more interesting stones for posterity although few now remain.

The oldest stone was a rough slab inscribed:

> '1675. Her lys JG. : I.M.'

The original benefactor of the land upon which the church and churchyard stands was Gabriel Norrie. Even in the Reverend Williams' time his gravestone was virtually unreadable but what could be made out said:

> 'Heir lyes Gabriel Norrie of Norriestoun who [   ] this lif the 13 [   ]
> ptr..81 and of his age f 47.

> he ever wys and prudent was
> At hom abrood as wis men knaws
> G.N. & U. [   ]'

Nearby is the gravestone of his wife:

> 'Margaret Forrester, Lady Norrie, who departed.......'

The rest of the stone is underground.

There were at least 5 or 6 other stones of the seventeenth century such as:

> 'her lys A.M.' and 'LS. MG' and 'Heir lyes Samuel Marjoribanks who
> departed this life the 14th day of march and of his age 28, 1690'

Our forefathers took some comfort from the lyrical inscriptions often carved upon their close relatives' gravestones. It is always so poignant to hear of the tragedies, often involving young children, which stared into the faces of our ancestors so often:

'Andrew Symers and Elizabeth Smith where lyes interd Elizabeth and
Andrew and Jean and Alexander Symers who died young, children of
theirs
heir lyes four blossoms early pued
Ever they came to their priem
Theirfor do you improve weaill
while you have precious time   1770'

A later Sommers' grave has an excellent pun:

'who needs a teacher to admonish him
That flesh is grass, that earthly things are mists?
What are our joys but dreams, and what our hopes
But goodly shadows in the summer's cloud

The modest grave of George McKerracher (hanged for forgery) and Agnes Fisher lay nearby, (although the stone has gone) as still does the grave of Duncan McLachlan, late of Macrieston who died in 1832. Duncan was the son of 'Duncan the Reiver'. We know little about him, but it is said that another of his sons went missing in the moss and his body was finally found by means of a dream of his sister that correctly identified his location.

A rather sombre message lay on the gravestone of John Smith:

'Heare lays the corps of John Bowie Smith, who departed this life Nov
21st 1791, aged 21 years'

On the reverse side could be read:

'O mortal man as you pass by
on this tombstone cast your eye
What you are now so once was I
my glass was run and yours is running
prepare for death, judgement is coming'

The Spittal family have a stone which records their names and goes on to read:

'stop stranger here and view
thy pictured fate however hon[or'd]
or however great all conquering
death without distinction brings
on equal footing humble men
and kings. on faith and virtue
then your hope must rest
being numbered with the truly best

135

A very touching inscription recorded the grave of Isabel Ramsay of Thornhill, who died aged 18 on the 4 July 1799:

'Boquhapple bred me, learning brought me, and Norrieston caught me. Labour pressed me, and sickness distressed me, and death oppressed me, and the grave possessed me. God first gave me, Christ died to save me, the earth did crave me and heaven would have me. Both old and young as you here pass me by, I desire while you ae all in life, to think on the state in which I now ly, for as you are so once was I, and now in the grave here ly'.

The McLarens' of Middleton have a large stone with many of their family recorded including the famous architect / designer of the village of Fortingall, James Marjoribanks McLaren who died in Hampstead aged 37.

Appendix 2: The Thornhill Piper

Once a familiar sight on entering Thornhill this poem was written to mark the sad occasion when the piping figure was taken away.

The ae leggit minstrel wha cheered Thornhill
The sough o' his reeds O, wae's me is still
Fareweel to the piper, they've ta'en him awa
Drone, chanter, bag, bonnet, feather an a'
Fareweel, fareweel to oor piper

The laddies threw stanes as they went by the hoose
Yet he never complained, or let his temper loose;
Wi a body roun' a fav'rite was he
we likit himsel' an' his sweet melodie
Fareweel, fareweel to oor piper

He aye played the tunes his hearers thocht best
pathetic or merry according to taste
An tho' some didna hear the music he played
Yet fretfu' remarks he never aince made
 Fareweel, fareweel to oor piper

They've ta'en him awa to a better place
Whar' we trust he'll be treated wi' kindly grace
Nae mair can the folks o' Thornhill dae
Than salute oor auld frien' wi R.I.P.
Fareweel, fareweel to oor piper

(anon.)

Appendix 3

Volunteers for active service from Thornhill and District in October 1914

(They were to be joined by many more as the war progressed)

Malcolm Baird	Royal Fusiliers
Colin Baird	Black Watch
John Bremner	Argyll and Sutherland Highlanders
James Brown	Black Watch
John Buchanan	Black Watch
James Buchanan	Black Watch
Alex Buchanan	Black Watch
John Campbell	Seaforth Highlanders
Robert Donaldson	Cameronians
Gilbert Hamilton	Highland Light Infantry
Milton Hamilton	Highland Light Infantry
John Hay	Black Watch
William Miller	Cameron Highlanders
Charles Moir	Black Watch
James Montgomery	Scottish Horse
Joseph Murray	Scottish Horse
Hugh Murray	Seaforth Highlanders
William Murray	5th Dragoon Guards
Alexander McDonald	Argyll and Sutherland Highlanders
Archibald McDonald	Scottish Horse
John McLachlan	Black Watch
John McKinley	Black Watch
Alexander McKenzie	Royal Navy
Gabriel Newton	Black Watch
John Rae	Argyll and Sutherland Highlanders
Peter Sinclair	Argyll and Sutherland Highlanders

Appendix 4: Kippen Jock

A poem to celebrate 'Kippen Jock' written by a person who knew him well

When Kippen Jock drave oot his yoke
Wi' her'n an' haddies laden
It was a joy to man and boy,
Douce matron and fair maiden;
But on that yoke, the canny folk,
Wad ne'er their ainsel's lippen
th'o a' agreed, Jock was, indeed,
the uncrowned king o' Kippen.

When Kippen Jock gaed on the troke,
wi' sheltie aft rebellin',
The baudrons kent the gate he went,
an' after him gaed yellin',
The wheels ungreased, baith whined and wheezed,
An' set the peesweeps skirlin',
till echoes broke on Kilmadock,
Syne back again on Stirlin'.

When Kippen Jock assessed his stock,
While on their highroad bauchlin',
The wheels had ne'er been meant to pair,
An fearsomely gaed shauchlin'.
The sheltie, tae, had ne'er a shae
an' stauchered in an odd way;
Sae wheels an' beast could wale, at least
The best bits o' the roadway.

When Kippen Jock o' riches spoke,
Twas never o' his ain gear;
For fortune aye bade him 'goodbye',
An passed him like a reindeer;
But still apace, he did her chase,
Yet what could be the sequel?
Jock's chariot, an' a' whatnot,
Were tae the task unequal.

When Kippen Jock, ae mornin' woke
Intil his breeks he sprauchled,
But plainly saw an end to't a',
An' couldna mair be trauchled.
For yokes an' men gang doon, an' then,
They canna mair be mended.
Sae this, I fear, like Jock's career,
Maun be untimely ended.

Anon.

Appendix 5: The Black Swans

The local ministers enjoyed a high profile in the village but the villagers were certainly not averse to subjecting them to mild teasing if the opportunity arose. The 'black swans' refer to the Established Church Minister the Rev Mitchell and the UF Church Minister the Rev Williams, both practising in the village in the early years of this century. The poem, reputedly written by Jock Ferguson the proprietor of the Crown Hotel, refers to the time when the ministers fell through the ice of the curling pond situated on the Lug in the North Common.

A pair o' swans fell on the 'lug'
and spoilt oor pond for curlin'
They spread their wings oot raither wide,
and through the ice gaed birlin'

You're aware they've awa' necks
Thats what kept them fleatin'
Had anither minute passed
They were at the bottom

A lucky thing that I was there
I couldna' hae been faster
had it not been for my pluck
Twa kirks withoot a Pastor

Ane was short an' ane was tall
The wee ane got the best o't
The wee ane landed tae the neck
The big ane got the rest o't

When we get them tae the shore
Hoo comical thay lookit
They shood their feathers in the sun
For they were fairly dreekit

The only cure we could apply
Altho' a little risky
Was Dr. William's Pink pills
And Mitchell's Irish Whiskey

When they found safe, they made for hame
But took anither track,
Instead o' merchin east the toun
They slippit roon' the back

Appendix 6

The Class of 1922:

L to R Back Row: Jean Douglas, Jessie Ferguson, Jean McFarlane, Dolly Steer, Mary McGowan, Cathy McGowan, Betty Spence
Third Row: Not known, Jimmy Douglas, John Donaldson, James Gilvear, John Jamieson, Harry Johnston, James Paterson, John Stewart, Mary McLay, Daisy McLauchlan.
Second Row: Mary Ann Newton, Donella Beaton, Flora Newton, Chrissie Ainslie, Mr. Kilgour (Headmaster), Rose Ainslie, Agnes Gray, Ella Spence
Front Row: David McAra, Jimmy Tetstal, George Steer, Jimy McPhee, Peter Buchanan

Appendix 7

Hearth Tax Lists 1694

Taxation rolls are particularly useful for recognising names in specific districts. The hearth tax ran from 1691 - 1695 and was imposed on those who had permanent dwellings. It gives the names of house occupants and the number of hearths possessed. It does not give any more detail about streets or individual houses.

It is particularly interesting to Thornhill as it gives a snapshot of the local residents in the years immediately preceding the feuing out of the village.

Only a selection of the occupants from outlying parts of Kincardine parish are given. The numbers represent the number of hearths in the house.

Lanrick   2 entries
Blairdrummond 7 entries
Burnbank   10 entries

Kings Boquhapple

Archibald Napier in Great House	6	William Mitchell and James Law	5
James Spittal and Hugh Patsone	3	Simson Humble and Andrew Mitchell	2
Jon Hardie and David Turner	3	Jon Morrison and James Steuart	3
Harie Graham	2		

Boquhapple (Govean)

Patrick McKerracher and John McCallan	4	James Jenkins and James Ferguson	3
Andrew McGowan and John Monteith	2	George Dow and Jon McGowan	2
John Mitchell and John Ferguson	2	Walter Paterson and Alex McLaren	2
Walter Howie and James Smyth	2	Duncan McArthur and Isobel Douglas	2
John Ferguson	3		

Norrieston

William McVey and Janet Spittal	2	John Alisone	1
Robert Muschet in manor house	3	George Harrison and Janet Dog	2
John Paterson and William Reoch	2	Elizabeth Spittal and Janet Backop	2
John Spittal and John Miller	2	Finlay Spittal and Donald McArthur	2
William Turner	1		

Bibliography

Note: SRO   Scottish Records Office, Edinburgh
       CRA   Central Region Archives
       PA   Perth Archives
       FNH   Forth Naturalist and Historian

ARCHAEOLOGICAL SITES AND MONUMENTS OF STIRLING DISTRICT   1979
BEAUCHAMP E   Braes of Balquidder   1978
CADEL   Story of the Forth   1913
CENSUS RETURNS   SRO   various
CENSUS SUMMARY VOLUME   PA   1851
CESS BOOKS   PA   1703 - 1719
COWBROUGH J G   Lodge Blairhoyle No. 792   1995
CUNNINGHAM - GRAHAM R.B.   Notes on the District of Menteith   1907
DIRECTORY OF FORMER SCOTTISH COMMONTIES   SRO
DIXON GEORGE A   Founding of Thornhill in 1696 FNH Vol 18 1995
DODGSHON R A   Land and Society in Early Scotland   1981
DRUMMOND WRITS AND ESTATE PAPERS   CRA   various
DRYSDALE WILLIAM   Old faces, Old Places and Old Stories of Stirling 1898
DRYSDALE WILLIAM   Auld Biggins of Stirling   1904
DUNCAN A A M   Making of the Kingdom   1975
EDINBURGH ALMANAC
FERGUSON   Tourist Guide to Callander and the Trossachs 1890
FORSYTH R   Beauties of Scotland vol. iv   1806
FRASER W   Red Book of Menteith   1880
GRAHAM P   General View of the Agriculture of Stirling 1812
GRAHAM P   Sketches Descriptive of Picturesque Scenery on the
                           Southern Confines of Perthshire   1806
HALDANE ARB   Drove Roads of Scotland   1973
HERON R   Scotland Delineated   1799
HOME DAVID   The Estuary of the Forth and adjoining Districts
                           viewed Geologically   1871
HUTCHISON A F   Lake of Menteith   1849
JOHNSTON B   Place Names of Scotland   1934
KILLEARN TRUST   The Parish of Killearn   1988
KINCARDINE IN MENTEITH   Kirk Session records   CRA   various
KING W   A Short History of the Church at Norrieston 1979
LINDSAY MAURICE   Lowland Scottish Villages   1980
MACKAY MORAY   Doune - Historic notes   1953
MARSHALL WILLIAM   Historic Scenes in Perthshire   1880
MCKEAN CHARLES   Stirling and the Trossachs   1985
MILLER   Handbook of Central Scotland   1883

MITCHELL S and MITCHELL J F	Monumental Inscriptions (prc - 1855) In South Perthshire		1974
MURRAY W H	Rob Roy MacGregor		1982
NAPIER MARK	Napier of Merchiston		1834
NEW STATISTICAL ACCOUNT	Parish of Kincardine		1844
NICLAISEN W	Scottish Place Names		1976
NORRIESTON KIRK SESSION RECORDS		CRA	various
NORRIESTON UF KIRK SESSION RECORDS		CRA	various
OLD STATISTICAL ACCOUNT OF SCOTLAND	Parish of Kincardine		791-1799
ROSS I S	Lord Kames and the Scotland of his day		1972
PATERSON P T	Bygone days in Cambusbarron		
PERTHSHIRE ADVERTISER	Know your county (July 31)		1990
RAMSAY J	(MSS of Ochtertyre) Scotland and Scotsmen of the 18th Century		1880
REGISTER OF SASINES		SRO	Various
SCOTT WALTER	Rob Roy		
SCOTTISH WOMEN'S RURAL INSTITUTE	Rural remembers 1925 - 1965		1965
SLATER	Directory		1860
SMITH C.A.	Life of Henry Home Drummond		
STEWART JAMES	Settlements of Western Perthshire		1990
STIRLING ANTIQUARY	Vol. 1 Various articles		1893
STIRLING JOURNAL AND ADVERTISER			1830 - 1960
STIRLING OBSERVER	1836 - 1986		
THIRD STATISTICAL ACCOUNT	Parish of Kincardine		1952
TRANS. ROYAL SOCIETY OF EDINBURGH (account of peat moss in Kincardine)			1794
TRANTER NIGEL	Queens Scotland -the Heartland		1971
TURNOCK D	Historic Geography of Scotland since 1707		1982
TYLER W	Military Roads of Scotland		1976
VALUATION ROLLS	W. Perthshire	PA.	Various
WEBSTER	A Census of Scotland (44) Scottish History Society		1755
WEST PERTHSHIRE DISTRICT COUNCIL RECORDS		CRA	Various
WHYTE I	Scotland before the Industrial Revolution		1995
WILLIAMS G (Rev)	Original Manuscripts c/o R. Dick		Various

Index